To the victims of terrorism
whose innocence was ripped
out of them with the unseeing
heartlessness of bomb shrapnel.

Boston's Bloody Marathon
by Tom Ramstack

© Copyright 2015 Tom Ramstack

ISBN 978-1-63393-144-2

All rights reserved. No part of this publication may be reproduced, stored in a retrieval system, or transmitted in any form or by any means – electronic, mechanical, photocopy, recording, or any other – except for brief quotations in printed reviews, without the prior written permission of the author.

Published By

THE LEGAL FORUM

In association with

köehlerstudios

Boston's Bloody Marathon

Tom Ramstack

Victims still lie at the site of one of the Boston Marathon bomb blasts on April 15, 2013.

Credit: Aaron "Tango" Tang, by Wikimedia Commons

The immediate aftermath of the Boston Marathon bombings.

Credit: Aaron "Tango" Tang, by Wikimedia Commons

Smoke still lingers immediately after one of the Boston Marathon explosions.

Credit: Aaron "Tango" Tang, by Wikimedia Commons

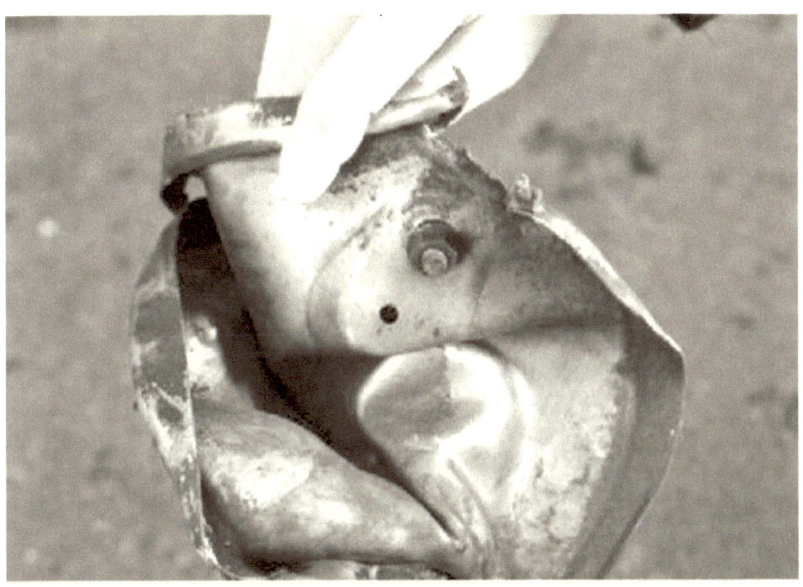

Shrapnel from one of the pressure cooker bombs at the Boston Marathon.

Credit: FBI, by Wikimedia Commons

Remnants of fireworks believed by the FBI to have been used by the Tsarnaev brothers to make bombs and displayed to the media on May 1, 2013.

Credit: FBI by Wikimedia Commons

A memorial at the site of the Boston Marathon bombings on July 30, 2013.

Credit: Ingfbruno, by Wikimedia Commons

A makeshift memorial in Copley Square, near the finish line of the Boston Marathon, on July 30, 2013.

Credit: Ingfbruno, by Wikimedia Commons

President Obama congratulates Massachusetts General Hospital staff on April 18, 2013 who cared for Boston Marathon bombing victims.

Credit: The White House, by Wikimedia Commons

Boston Police Commissioner Ed Davis at a press conference after the bombings on April 15, 2013.

Credit: Michael Cummo Photography, by Wikimedia Commons

Dzhokhar Tsarnaev

Credit: VOA, by Wikimedia Commons

Tamerlan Tsarnaev, who is accused of being a domineering and malevolent influence over his younger brother, Dzhokhar.

Credit:
U.S. Public Defender Service.

Dzhokhar Tsarnaev shows disrespect to a jailhouse video camera three months after he was incarcerated.

Credit:
U.S. Attorney's Office

Dzhokhar and Tamerlan Tsarnaev at the Boston Marathon on April 15, 2013 minutes before they detonate explosives.

Credit: FBI

Table of Contents

A Mangled Marathon 5
An Emergency Response 14
The Investigation Begins 18
Tamerlan Tsarnaev 26
Dzhokhar Tsarnaev 39
The Chase is On 48
A Night of Guns 50
End of the Road for the Tsarnaevs 59
The Lawyers and Judges Take Over 69
Dzhokhar Makes a Court Appearance 73
A Murder Investigation Reopens 81
The Death Penalty 87
Tamerlan's Widow 95
Friends Forever 100
Congress Demands Answers 103

Homegrown Terrorism Takes Root 111

The Rogues Gallery. 121

Al Qaeda Takes the Lead 133

ISIS Sees an Opportunity. 141

Jury Selection Begins 151

The Opening Statements 165

The Prosecution's Witnesses 171

The Defense Tries Its Best. 184

A Life on the Line. 193

The Defense's Last-Ditch Effort 199

Verdict. 209

Note to the Reader

Although this book focuses on the April 15, 2013 bombings at the Boston Marathon, its victims and the prosecution of the prime suspect, it is equally about "lone wolf" terrorists. Lone wolves refer to terrorists who plot their attacks alone, usually with no organization to support them and no official links to violent groups. There is almost no way to know their next target until they strike. U.S. intelligence agencies call them perhaps the biggest terrorist threat to the United States and its allies. They also say the threat is growing as the U.S. military and its allies dismantle the most deadly terrorist organizations, forcing them to turn to lone wolves to continue their violent campaigns.

A MANGLED MARATHON

ON A BRISK April 15, 2013 morning, the annual running of the Boston Marathon started with no hint of the tragedy that would befall it hours later.

Hundreds of thousands of spectators lined the 26.2-mile trek to Boston's Back Bay on a bright, shiny day, ready to hand the runners cups of water and to cheer them toward the finish line.

The announcer at the starting line in Hopkinton asked for a moment of silence to honor victims of the Sandy Hook Elementary School shooting in nearby Newtown, Connecticut that claimed the lives of 26 persons four months earlier.

It was the work of a madman with a gun, according to press reports.

After the 26-second pause for the fallen, America's oldest public marathon began with 52 wheelchair-bound racers giving the first spins to their wheels at 9:17 a.m. They were followed by 51 elite women runners — selected as some of the world's best marathoners — at 9:30 a.m. Next came elite men at 10 a.m.

The remaining roughly 23,200 competitors from across the United States and 92 countries were released in three waves over the next 40 minutes.

Among them was a 57-year-old mother from Maryland named Carol. Her surname, along with those of her family members, are omitted to protect their privacy.

As usual, the Kenyans and Ethiopians set the pace, finishing two hours ahead of most competitors. The first three runners to cross the finish line for both elite men and elite women were from Kenya and Ethiopia. The first Americans finished fourth in both men's and women's divisions.

The only American to claim a first place prize was Tatyana McFadden, who won in the women's wheelchair race.

But before the race was over, few people cared who won or lost. Boston's Patriots Day, a day of festivities to celebrate the American Revolution, was about to become the latest nightmare in America's ongoing war on terrorism.

At 2:50 pm, as the biggest chunk of racers approached the finish line, a bomb concealed in a backpack exploded on the sidewalk nearby. It was followed 13 seconds later by another concealed bomb on the sidewalk only 210 yards away on Boylston Street.

The blast prompted widespread screaming and spectators to run for cover. Windows shattered in nearby buildings while two large puffs of white smoke billowed upward over Copley Square.

One witness told CNN, "It felt like a huge cannon."

Three people were killed almost immediately. Another 264 were injured, 14 of whom required amputations.

A Florida trauma care doctor who was watching the race as a spectator described for national television networks what he saw as he approached the "mangled" blast site.

"I saw at least six to seven people down next to me," he said. "They protected me from the blast. One lady expired. One gentleman lost both his (lower) limbs. Most of the injuries were lower extremities."

Some witnesses told about a man who lost his legs not fully

understanding what had happened as he struggled to stand on feet only barely attached to the rest of his body.

The pungent smell of gunpowder hung in the air while shrapnel, ball bearings and nails littered the streets near the blast sites. Spectators left behind backpacks, cellphones and handmade signs with runners' names.

Doctors at Brigham and Women's Hospital later treated one patient whose body had been pierced by 12 carpenter's nails.

Cellphone and surveillance camera video of the moment of detonation show 78-year-old Bill Iffrig, a veteran marathoner, running in the street near the finish line. As the first bomb exploded, "the shock waves just hit my whole body and my legs just started jittering around," he told reporters.

The video shows Iffrig falling to the ground while wearing his running shorts and an orange tank top. An event volunteer stepped up to help him to his feet.

Iffrig suffered only a minor scratch.

At first many of the runners speculated that it was an electrical explosion. Moments later they realized it was a bomb.

Carol's daughters, Erika and Nicole, along with son-in-law Michael, stood near the finish line, waiting for Carol to cross it.

Instead, shrapnel from the first blast ripped into the bodies of Erika, Nicole and Michael.

Michael suffered lacerations to his upper body. Nicole's legs were severely injured.

Erika, a 29-year-old preschool teacher, suffered the worst of the injuries.

A day before the marathon, she was doing homework for a master's degree in early childhood education she sought at a Maryland university. The day of the marathon, she had a good view of the finish line to watch her mother complete the race.

Unlike some survivors whose injuries left them with no clear memory of the explosion, Erika remembered nearly everything, right up to the time an anesthesia mask was put over her face in the emergency department of Beth Israel Deaconess Medical Center.

As the first bomb detonated, she remembers seeing flashes of orange and yellow. She didn't hear the blast because her eardrums were perforated by the explosion. She was knocked to the pavement.

Her left foot would not move. In a later news media interview, she said, "I'm lying there and I have this horrible moment that I'm going to die. I had a conversation with God. I said, 'I'm not ready to go. I'm not done yet.'"

An uninjured bystander approached, introducing herself as Joan from California and saying she was there to help. She gave a belt to an emergency medical technician who used it as a tourniquet around Erika's leg, perhaps saving her life as she bled profusely.

Within minutes, the streets filled with stretchers and wheelchairs as ambulances crowded the neighborhood for blocks around.

Erika screamed for her sister and brother-in-law but received no reply.

While still lying on the pavement, she grabbed her purse, glasses and Kindle e-reader before being loaded onto an ambulance gurney. Her camera still was strapped around one wrist.

Emergency medical technicians put her into the ambulance beside another seriously injured woman. One of the EMTs described the women as "criticals" who needed to be immediately transported to a hospital.

Erika was wheeled straight to an operating room, where surgical personnel cut her clothes off, including her Baltimore Ravens shirt.

Then she remembers the anesthesia mask over her face. Then she remembers waking up in the intensive care unit.

By the time her mother arrived at Beth Israel Deaconess,

Erika's left leg was amputated below the knee. Her mother was one of the first to speak with her after she revived.

Carol said her daughter's first question was, "What happened to Nicole and Michael?" Next she asked, "What did they tell my kids?" Finally she asked, "What happened to my leg?"

Following the first amputation, doctors cut off more of her left leg above the knee as Erika suffered painful spasms and her medical team determined the leg could not be saved.

Her right leg required muscle and skin grafts and insertion of a rod to stabilize it. The leg was scarred from burns.

Erika would be the last of the bombing victims to leave the hospital, spending 50 days confined to her sixth-floor room. Twenty-seven hospitals participated in treating the bomb victims.

"It's going to be a long, long road," Carol's husband told ABC News. "At least everybody in our family is alive."

During a Nov. 8, 2013 appearance on the ABC television show "The View," she demonstrated her hesitant and halting ability to get up from her wheelchair and walk with a prosthetic leg as the audience applauded.

* * *

Down the street from Erika when the second bomb detonated stood a married couple named Adrianne, 32, and Adam, 33.

The couple attended the marathon as spectators. It was one of Adam's first social events since returning from Afghanistan, where he served in the Air Force.

They had planned to spend Patriots Day shopping and watching the end of the marathon.

The blast knocked the couple to the pavement where they fell on top of each other.

"I said my foot hurt, and he held up my foot, and we both just screamed bloody murder," Adrianne said in an interview with local media in Boston.

They crawled into a nearby restaurant. Her husband used

his belt as a tourniquet around his wife's leg as she asked him to tighten it, hoping a tight squeeze would diminish the pain.

Other spectators rushed in to help the injured married couple before they were carried away in an ambulance.

Doctors were unable to save her left foot. They also removed part of her left leg below the calf.

Until the blast, she worked as a dance instructor at Arthur Murray Studios in Boston.

Her husband suffered a perforated eardrum. Shrapnel cut a nerve and artery in his left foot. His right foot needed a graft from his thigh to repair torn skin and muscles.

Adrianne's mother broke the news to her daughter as she woke up in a Boston Medical Center hospital room after surgery.

Adrianne asked her mother to help her move her left foot. Her mother told her she had no left foot.

Adrianne responded by punching her pillow, throwing a water bottle and sheets.

While she still awaited a prosthetic leg, she pledged to herself that she would dance again, perhaps even run the marathon.

* * *

An image that came to symbolize the tragedy of the marathon bombings emerged from a family photograph of 8-year-old Martin Richard, who was one of three people killed by the blasts.

His mother, father and sister were seriously injured. Their 7-year-old daughter lost a leg.

The photograph taken before the marathon shows Martin holding up a drawing he made with crayons. At the top it says, "No more hurting people." Below the sentence, he wrote "Peace" in multi-colored lettering with hearts on each side of the word and a peace sign drawn at the bottom.

Martin, who was known for liking knock-knock jokes and math games, is shown looking at the camera with a half-smile and a missing baby tooth.

"My dear son Martin has died from injuries sustained in the attack on Boston," the boy's father said in a statement. "My wife and daughter are both recovering from serious injuries. We thank our family and friends, those we know and those we have never met, for their thoughts and prayers. I ask that you continue to pray for my family as we remember Martin."

Martin's father, a respected civic activist in Boston, suffered shrapnel wounds to his legs.

The family went to the marathon to participate in what has become a Boston tradition: celebrating the beginning of warmer weather while watching one of the nation's most famous races.

Martin's family originally watched the race several blocks away from the blast site near Hereford Street. They were watching for neighbors they knew were running the race.

They left their vantage point to buy ice cream, then returned to a spot closer to the finish line. After 15 minutes of watching sometimes bedraggled runners end the race, the first explosion hit them.

A bystander who came to help Martin's sister moments later was quoted by local television station WCVB saying, "I saw her laying in the street. I held her head in my hands and I tried to rub her and comfort her.

"She was just a baby and so badly injured and scared," the bystander said. "But she was so incredibly brave. I saw him [Martin] and at that point I knew he was gone. I'll never forget them. That little girl, she was so brave."

Martin's family put out a public statement May 9 to respond to inquiries about their progress. It included several sentences about their daughter, who underwent 11 surgeries in 23 days.

"After not being able to communicate with [our daughter] for the first two weeks, she woke up with difficult questions that needed to be answered," the family's statement said. "There are not words to describe how hard sharing this heartbreaking news was on all of us."

Martin's schoolmates drew a makeshift memorial to the third grader in chalk on the pavement at Hemenway Park, where he and his friends from Neighborhood House Charter School would play.

"Pray for Martin," said one of the messages written in pink chalk. Other messages pledged they would never forget him.

* * *

The other fatalities were identified as 29-year-old restaurant worker Krystle Campbell and 23-year-old Boston University graduate student Lingzi Lu.

Beth Roche, an Indiana woman who was watching her daughter finish the marathon, remembers her injury vividly.

"My knee opened up like a sardine can," she said. "Everything now in slow motion. I was lying on the ground and people were walking over me to get into [the] marathon shoe store. The last thing I saw before feeling alone was blood trickling down the leg of a girl that was going in the store."

A police officer arrived. She was moved first to a triage tent, then an ambulance and finally Tufts Medical Center.

As the physical pain of the bombings subsided, Roche and other victims dealt with psychological struggles.

After returning home and receiving her third surgery on Oct. 23, 2013, she said, "I am determined and positive most of the time but this last surgery has really challenged my will and soul. I am still fighting with the help of [physical therapy]...

"As far as the terrorist, I have no comment other than I feel he will have to face the consequences of his actions," she said.

* * *

Sarah Girouard, a college student from Maine who suffered serious leg injuries in the bombing, said for this report, "I don't know if you can call it a coping mechanism or not but soon after it happened, I tried not to get emotionally attached to the event —as impossible as that may sound. I don't have much animosity toward them because I think I've emotionally disassociated myself away from this event so much in order to stay strong."

As the victims and their friends spoke about coping with tragedy, police and lawmakers were promising that someone would pay dearly for the crime.

President Barack Obama issued a statement shortly after the bombings saying, "Any responsible individuals, any responsible groups, will feel the full weight of justice."

AN EMERGENCY RESPONSE

ALTHOUGH THE MARATHON bombings surprised nearly everyone, they did not catch Boston unprepared.

Many rescue and medical workers already waited nearby to care for any of the thousands of runners and spectators who might become sick or get injured during the race.

Police immediately stopped the race. They diverted the remaining runners away from the finish line toward Boston Common and Kenmore Square.

Buildings around Copley Square, including the Lenox Hotel, were evacuated. Police shut down a 15-square-block area around the blast site. They were assisted by Massachusetts Army National Guard soldiers, who also helped injured victims.

Boston Police Commissioner Ed Davis recommended that residents stay off the streets in case the bombs were only a portion of a larger attack.

"The carnage was terrible," Davis said during a press conference. "Body parts, amputations. Over 35 years, I've seen a lot but I have never, ever seen anything like this, and I hope I never do again."

The initial press reports implied more explosions were possible as police checked abandoned backpacks on streets, similar to the ones that concealed the first two bombs.

Firefighters who erroneously believed another bomb might be concealed under the grandstand stayed at a distance while aiming fire hoses at it.

Police called in bomb squads to check each of the bags. They found one bag they believed contained a bomb. They announced they would detonate a controlled explosion in the 600 block of Boylston Street to get rid of the potential bomb before it hurt someone.

After their detonation they discovered they had just destroyed someone's harmless abandoned bag.

The Navy sent a bomb disposal unit to Boston to help the police but no other explosive devices were found.

By that time, images of another organized, well-planned plot — similar to the 2001 September 11 attack that killed about 3,000 Americans — were racing through the heads of emergency preparedness personnel in Massachusetts and elsewhere.

Locally, the Massachusetts Bay Transportation Authority shut down some of its transit service. The shutdown was based on intelligence reports that show passenger trains and buses are prime targets for terrorists, particularly when bombs are used for widespread death and destruction.

As word spread through the airwaves about the bombings, cellphone service in the Boston area became jammed by callers checking on friends and family members. The Massachusetts Emergency Management Agency recommended that cellphone customers use text messaging instead of voice service.

Some local media outlets incorrectly reported that cellphone service was shut down to prevent terrorists from remotely detonating bombs. Cellphone service continued operating but with slowed or delayed access.

The Boston Police Department tried to ease concerns by

setting up a helpline to allow callers to check on whether friends or family members might be among the injured. The helpline requested information from anyone who had tips on who was hurt ... and who might be responsible. All off-duty Boston police were asked to report for duty.

The American Red Cross sent its personnel to compile a list of the injured and to inform their families. The Red Cross also sent extra blood donation packets to Boston hospitals. Google Person Finder activated its emergency Internet service that provided online updates about the bombings and its victims under the log-on phrase of "Boston Marathon Explosions."

As far away as Los Angeles, San Francisco and Seattle, police announced they were putting their officers on heightened alert.

The Los Angeles police department put out an announcement repeating their advice to the public: "If you see something, say something."

In New York, Mayor Michael Bloomberg said the city had about 1,000 officers trained in counterterrorism tactics, "and they — along with the entire NYPD and the investments we have made in counterterrorism infrastructure — are being fully mobilized to protect our city."

The federal government's response began minutes after the explosions, about the same time FBI Director Robert Mueller briefed President Obama.

The Federal Aviation Administration restricted the airspace over Boston by forbidding pilots from flying less than three miles high over the blast site. The restriction later was reduced to two miles. The FAA also put a brief temporary ground stop on flights out of the city's Logan International Airport.

U.S. Attorney General Eric Holder announced the Justice Department would direct all its efforts at investigating the crime and prosecuting the persons responsible.

He and the FBI's Mueller agreed that Carmen Ortiz, the U.S. Attorney for the District of Massachusetts, should coordinate the response of the Justice Department, the FBI, the Bureau of Alcohol, Tobacco, Firearms and Explosives and other law enforcement agencies.

An Obama administration official quoted Homeland Security Secretary Janet Napolitano saying she had ordered her department to provide "whatever assistance is necessary" to state and local authorities in Massachusetts.

As word of the tragedy spread to Congress, the House of Representatives held a minute of silence to honor the blast victims.

Obama addressed the nation just after 6 p.m., saying the "full resources" of the federal government would be aimed at finding the persons responsible.

"Today is a holiday in Massachusetts, Patriots Day," the president said in a televised statement. "It's a day that celebrates the free and fiercely independent spirit that this great American city of Boston has reflected from the earliest days of our nation, and it's a day that draws the world to Boston's streets in a spirit of friendly competition ... The American people will say a prayer for Boston tonight."

Other condolences came from Canadian Prime Minister Stephen Harper, who said, "It is truly a sad day when an event as inspiring as the Boston Marathon is clouded by such senseless violence."

British Foreign Secretary William Hague said he was "appalled" by the attack.

THE INVESTIGATION BEGINS

AS THE INVESTIGATION started, the FBI and police were pursuing their assumption that Boston was targeted by what U.S. Rep. Bill Keating of Massachusetts called a "sophisticated, coordinated, planned attack."

Adding to the mystery was the fact that state and federal officials said they had no hint before the explosions that the marathon might be targeted, despite a multi-billion dollar state and federal network to stop terrorists.

In Congress, Rep. Peter King, a member of the House Intelligence Committee, said, "I received two top secret briefings last week on the current threat levels in the United States, and there was no evidence of this at all."

The FBI led the investigation that soon was joined by the Central Intelligence Agency, the National Counterterrorism Center and the Drug Enforcement Administration.

The team of investigators grew to about 1,000 officers.

Bloody clothes, shoes, bags and other personal items retrieved from the scene began accumulating in an unmanageable mess. They were followed by thousands of photographs and videos.

Boylston Street, normally a lively Boston neighborhood, had

been transformed into the biggest crime scene in Massachusetts' history.

Police used orange paint to map part of the 15-block area that had been cordoned off into a grid of rectangles. Each one was assigned a number that was matched to evidence found within it.

The FBI rented a warehouse in Boston's Seaport district as the depot for the evidence. Half the floor was covered with bloody clothing left to dry as FBI lab technicians arrived from their headquarters in Quantico, Virginia to analyze it.

In the other half of the warehouse floor, investigators quickly assembled a group to review the photographs and video for anything suspicious.

One FBI agent reported that he watched the same portion of a video about 400 times as investigators assembled a timeline of images. They tried to follow anyone who might be a suspect through a patchwork of photographs and video to shed light on their motives.

The first advisory to police from federal investigators asked them to watch for a "darker-skinned or black male" who might have a foreign accent. The advisory said the unidentified man was seen wearing a sweatshirt and black backpack. Witnesses said he was trying to get into a restricted area at the marathon about five minutes before the first explosion.

With no specific suspect in mind, police began questioning everyone they thought might have any clues.

One of them was a Saudi national who was hospitalized in Boston with a leg wound from the bombings. He was under guard but not in custody. Investigators acknowledged they had no evidence he participated in the bombings, only that he met the generalized description of a possible suspect.

He soon was cleared of any wrongdoing.

In another case of misidentification, the New York Post published a photograph of two people on its front page under the headline "Bagmen." Investigators determined they had nothing to do with the bombings.

As the emergency response faded, the FBI began issuing subpoenas for surveillance cameras around Copley Square as well as records from nearby cellphone towers. They reviewed the camera footage for incriminating images. They searched through cellphone records to trace calls made around the time of the explosions.

They also tried to recover pieces of the exploded bombs for the possible signature of the bombers the material might contain. Examples could include fingerprints and bomb components that lead only to one person or group.

Their search turned up nails, ball bearings, pieces of metal and black nylon from a backpack. The lid of a pressure cooker was found on a rooftop near the blast site. The FBI reconstructed some pieces of metal to conclude they were torn from two pressure cookers, each big enough to hold 1.5 gallons of fluid, or perhaps a bomb.

The remnants of a circuit board and wiring were spread out in pieces around the area.

All the evidence was sent to the national FBI laboratory in Quantico, Virginia. An initial examination showed no C-4, nitroglycerine or other military-style explosives, indicating the bombers assembled a crude explosive device.

Remnants of the explosive chemicals indicated it was the same kind of black powder material commonly found in over-the-counter fireworks. One government official told the Boston news media that smoke from the blasts was consistent with a "low-velocity improvised explosive mixture, perhaps flash powder or sugar chlorate mixture."

On April 24, the FBI and Homeland Security Department issued a bulletin that concluded the homemade bombs were detonated remotely with the kind of transmitter commonly used to guide battery-operated toy cars.

"Based on preliminary analysis of recovered evidence, each device likely incorporated an electrical fusing system using components from remote control toy cars, such as a transmitter and receiver pair operating at 2.4 GHz, an electronic speed control used as the switch mechanism and sub-C rechargeable battery packs at the power source," the bulletin said.

Even more disturbing was the fact the explosives packed in pressure cookers and detonators closely resembled the bomb designs described in the radical Islamist online magazine "Inspire."

A similar design is used to make what the U.S. military calls "improvised explosive devices," or IEDs. Islamist militants in Iraq and Afghanistan use them to blow up Humvee vehicles, as well as to blast the limbs off their occupants.

As the dust and debris in Boston settled, speculation swirled about whether Islamist terrorists should be blamed.

FBI and CIA terrorism expert Jeff Beatty said in a television interview with CNN that pressure cookers can be "very effective" casings for improvised bombs.

But he added, "That doesn't mean it was the Taliban. Other people can read about this."

Some lawmakers tried to downplay an Islamist connection until more evidence could be amassed.

Senator Saxby Chambliss, the Senate Intelligence Committee's ranking Republican, told reporters in Washington, "There are a lot of things that are surrounding this that would give an indication that it may have been a domestic terrorist, but that just can't be assumed."

"This is a very fluid investigation," he added.

U.S. Rep. Mike McCaul, chairman of the House Homeland Security Committee, updated the media as the investigation was starting by saying, "We don't know whether this was a homegrown terrorist or part of a wider conspiracy."

Homeland Security Secretary Janet Napolitano said there

was no evidence the Boston bombings were part of "a broader plot."

FBI agents began reading through jihadist web sites to see whether any Islamist groups claimed responsibility for the explosions, but found nothing that would help their investigation.

Federal officials also put out a call to members of the public who might have inadvertently filmed something important with their mobile phones or cameras.

"People don't know that they were witnesses, that they might actually have evidence in their phones or in their cameras," said Juliette Kayyem, the Obama administration's former assistant secretary for homeland security, on CNN's "Starting Point."

Among the suspicious photos were two broadcast by Boston's WHDH television station. One showed a bag on the ground beside a mailbox. The other showed the same spot moments later, with damage from the blast centered where the bag had been placed. The bag was no longer there.

Another photograph obtained by the FBI taken moments before the blast shows Martin Richard standing up against a barrier that separated spectators from runners in the street. His family members stood behind him and next to him.

Also standing behind him and to his left can be seen a young man with a Middle Eastern appearance wearing a white baseball cap turned backward on his head. The backpack that concealed the first bomb rested on the ground near him.

In the same photograph, Martin's sister is seen standing near him just before the explosion damaged her left leg so badly it required amputation.

But it was the man in the white cap who attracted the most attention among investigators. He fit the profile of the most likely suspects almost perfectly.

One set of images was the most telling of all, providing the smoking gun evidence that makes or breaks a criminal case.

It showed the man in the white hat setting his backpack

down outside the Forum restaurant then walking away.

On April 18, the FBI and Boston police held a press conference to ask the public's assistance to identify the man in the white cap, along with a companion, who were both photographed and captured in video images.

The images showed two men, both wearing caps, jackets and backpacks. They walked one behind the other along the sidewalk as the crowd of spectators stood near them watching the runners near the marathon finish line.

Nothing about their nonchalant demeanor gave a hint of anything out of the ordinary. At one point, the man in the white hat turned his cap around on his head in a way that gave cameras a clear look at his face. The man in the black hat can be seen speaking on his cellphone but showing no emotion when the first bomb exploded.

The FBI normally would have kept the photographs within their circle of investigators but decided to release them publicly to stem the backlash against innocent persons who were falling under suspicion.

"For more than 100 years, the FBI has relied on the public to be its eyes and ears," Richard DesLauriers, the FBI's special agent in charge of its Boston division, said at the 5 p.m. press conference. "With the media's help, in an instant, these images will be delivered directly into the hands of millions around the world. We know the public will play a critical role in identifying and locating them.

"Somebody out there knows these individuals as friends, neighbors, co-workers, or family members of the suspects. Though it may be difficult, the nation is counting on those with information to come forward.

"No bit of information, no matter how small or seemingly inconsequential, is too small. Each piece moves us forward towards justice," he said.

DesLauriers said the two suspects should be considered

armed and "extremely dangerous."

"No one should approach them," he said. "No one should attempt to apprehend them except law enforcement."

The FBI referred to the men in the photograph as Suspect 1 and Suspect 2, also as "black hat" and "white hat." Witnesses who saw them said they "acted differently" from most spectators.

The fact that many spectators fled the scene in surprise and shock made getting their testimony more difficult as the investigation started.

Witnesses said the two suspects hung around after the blasts. They stayed to watch the reaction of the crowd then walked away "casually," the FBI agents said.

More evidence came from 27-year-old Jeffrey Bauman, who lost both legs in the explosion. He was waiting for his girlfriend to cross the finish when he was hit with a blast.

After he regained consciousness at Boston Medical Center, he asked for a pen and paper. While still groggy from anesthesia, he wrote a note to the FBI that said, "Bag. Saw the guy, looked right at me."

The "guy" he mentioned set his bag down beside Bauman about two-and-a-half minutes before it exploded. His identification became crucial in the FBI's response.

The public release of the photographs and video provided the turning point in the investigation the FBI sought. It was followed by a deluge of other photographs, video camera images and witness testimony that described the same two suspects.

By the same evening as the May 18 press conference, the FBI received what one of its agents called a "large volume of calls" that he credited to the photographs. The FBI's web site was overwhelmed with a record number of emails.

The same day, President Obama tried to reassure Bostonians by attending a memorial service at the city's Cathedral of the Holy Cross.

The then-unknown persons who set the bombs "picked the wrong city," Obama told the audience. "Every one of us stands with you. Boston may be your hometown, but we claim it too ... For millions of us, what happened on Monday is personal."

He also directed a warning to the bombers.

"Yes, we will find you," he said. "And yes, you will face justice. We will hold you accountable."

Unfortunately for the suspects, they had chosen to set a bomb in the same metropolitan area where they resided, which made it easy for Bostonians to identify them.

"Black cap" was 26-year-old Tamerlan Tsarnaev. "White cap" was his 19-year-old brother Dzhokhar Tsarnaev. They came from a Muslim refugee family that had immigrated to the United States from Russia in 2002.

TAMERLAN TSARNAEV

TAMERLAN ANZOROVICH TSARNAEV was born Oct. 21, 1986 in the Kalmyk Autonomous Soviet Socialist Republic, in what is now the North Caucasus region of Russia.

The Tsarnaevs sometimes felt the brunt of discrimination as ethnic Chechens living in Kyrgyzstan while their native Chechnya was embroiled in wars against the Russian government. The separatist rebellion was smashed under the administrations of Russian presidents Boris Yeltsin and Vladimir Putin.

A contributing factor in the rebellion and the discrimination was the Islamic tradition commonly found among Chechens.

The Tsarnaev family, which included two boys and two girls, moved around within Russia several times. In the early 1990s, they settled in the boyhood home of Tamerlan's father, Anzor, in the Central Asian republic of Kyrgyzstan. The Tsarnaevs later moved to the children's mother's home near Makhachkala, the capital of Dagestan, before immigrating to the United States.

Anzor showed no obvious signs of the radical Islam that appeared to motivate his sons to set bombs at the Boston Marathon. His mother, Zubeidat, a Russian Avar from Chechnya, came from a region where women rarely wore pants and more commonly wore hijabs. Zubeidat, however, wore a modern hairstyle after moving to the United States and often dressed like any American woman, sometimes with jeans and high heels.

Anzor was studying law in Kyrgyzstan when the couple married in 1986. He later took a job as an investigator in the prosecutor's office in the city of Bishkek. The family lived about 40 miles away near a sugar factory in the small town of Tokmok.

A former neighbor described the Tsarnaev family as intelligentsia. One of Dzhokhar and Tamerlan's aunts was a lawyer.

Although Anzor held a good job, it could not last at a time of political reprisal against Chechens. After Russia invaded Chechnya in 1999, Anzor was fired during a purge of Chechens in the government of Kyrgyzstan.

The family fled first to Dagestan, but the civil war followed them. The Tsarnaev parents then decided to flee in 2002 to the United States, where Anzor's brother, Ruslan, was carving out an upper-middle class lifestyle as an attorney.

Tamerlan's parents and younger brother immigrated to the United States first. Tamerlan followed a year later, finishing high school at the public Cambridge Rindge and Latin School.

The U.S. government granted them permanent residence in March 2007, based in part on their refugee status.

At the time, the family lived in a low-income neighborhood in between Boston's Cambridge and Somerville suburbs.

Money was a persistent problem for them. They lived on public assistance in a multi-family house.

Anzor was known as a good auto mechanic, but still had difficulty finding jobs. He sometimes fixed cars on the street for $10 an hour, which met with complaints by neighbors. He would work without gloves even in the worst chill of the Massachusetts winters. Neighbors said his knuckles bulged from arthritis.

The financial problems seemed to aggravate a rift between

the Tsarnaev parents that ended with them separating. Anzor returned to Russia in failing health.

During his senior year of high school, Tamerlan became interested in boxing, which also gained him a small degree of notoriety in the Boston area.

After high school, he applied to the University of Massachusetts at Boston with plans to begin in the fall of 2006. He was rejected, which compelled him to attend Bunker Hill Community College instead.

For three semesters, he studied accounting as a part-time student at the community college with a goal of eventually becoming an engineer. He sometimes worked as a lifeguard for his primary income source.

Although he was known as a good student, he dropped out of the school in 2008 as he struggled with a shortfall of money to fund his education.

As he tried to find a steady job, Tamerlan spent much of his time training to box as a Golden Gloves contender.

In a 2009 sports article, the Lowell Sun wrote: "In Team New England's last bout of the night, Tamerlan Tsarnaev dropped a controversial decision to Lamar Fenner of Chicago in the 201-pound division.

"After flooring Fenner with a huge punch that required an eight-count, it seemed that Tsarnaev was in control of the whole fight.

"Yet somehow the judges saw it differently and awarded Fenner the decision, a decision that drew boos from the crowd.

"Team New England finished the first day of action with two wins and two losses."

Shortly afterward, Tamerlan won the New England Golden Gloves heavyweight championship and the Rocky Marciano Trophy.

About the same time, Tamerlan began speaking openly about his ambitions to box for the United States in the Olympics.

Also about that time, other people started noticing changes in Tamerlan. Among the changes was a growing disillusionment with the United States.

He was quoted in the Lowell Sun newspaper in 2004 shortly after his arrival in the United States for a story about a boxing tournament.

"I like the USA," Tamerlan said. "America has a lot of jobs."

But by 2010, when he was quoted in a Boston University publication called The Comment that included a photo layout of him, Tamerlan's attitude toward the United States seemed to be shifting. "I don't have a single American friend," he said. "I don't understand them."

One of the obvious changes that occurred in the interim was that Tamerlan had converted to Islam.

More than a preference for a specific religious denomination, Tamerlan was devout even by Muslim standards.

In the photo layout in The Comment, he explained why he did not smoke or drink alcohol. "God said no alcohol," he said.

He also said he rarely took off his shirt if women were in the Wai Kru Mixed Martial Arts Center in Boston where he trained so they would not get the wrong idea about him. "I'm very religious," he said.

Other statements by Tamerlan were more trivial, such as saying he liked the movie Borat, that he sometimes dressed European style and that kickboxers "don't know how to move."

He attended the Islamic Society of Boston mosque near his home in Cambridge, which was rumored in the local community to be a hotbed of militant Muslims.

The Boston-based nonprofit political advocacy group Americans for Peace and Tolerance said members of the mosque supported "a brand of Islamic thought that encourages grievance against the West, distrust of law enforcement and opposition to Western forms of government, dress and social values."

The group also alleges the $15.6 million mosque and Islamic cultural center is supported by Muslim extremists.

Tamerlan's devotion to Islam increasingly took on the same belligerence he brought into the boxing ring.

He once punched a Brazilian youth in the face who had dated his younger sister, Bella, for two years. Tamerlan did not approve of the relationship because the boy was not a Muslim, according to friends who knew the young couple.

On another occasion, Tamerlan rebuked a Middle Eastern grocery shopkeeper in Cambridge who advertised Thanksgiving turkeys.

"This is kuffar," the shopkeeper quoted him as saying in the local media. "Kuffar" is an Arabic word for non-Muslims.

"That's not right," Tamerlan reportedly said.

He also was known for being occasionally abusive toward a former girlfriend, whom he admitted to police he slapped in a July 28, 2009 incident. He was arrested for domestic assault and battery but the charges later were dismissed. He spent about half an hour in a local holding cell.

One of the issues in the dispute was the girlfriend's reluctance to convert to Islam and to wear traditional Muslim dress. The girlfriend described Tamerlan as a radical.

The girl called 9-1-1 "crying hysterically," police reported. She said her boyfriend beat her up. She also accused him of cheating on her with a Boston college student, who he later married.

The fight with the girlfriend was the only incident that ever drew suspicion from police before the marathon bombings.

"The only interaction we had with the Tsarnaevs was that 2009 arrest of Tamerlan," Dan Riviello, Cambridge Police Department spokesman, said for this report. "There just weren't a lot of indications out there."

Now, Boston area police are more "vigilant" about watching for anyone with violent tendencies similar to Tamerlan, Riviello said. "I think we're all doing a better job of sharing information between agencies," he said.

Tsarnaev family members said Tamerlan's radicalization started in late 2008 or early 2009 when he fell under the influence of a Muslim convert from nearby Rhode Island known as "Misha."

Before meeting Misha at the mosque, Tamerlan was mostly apathetic toward religion.

After being tutored by Misha, Tamerlan gave up his ambitions of being a music producer, saying Islam doctrine did not support it, according to family members. He became outspoken against the U.S. war efforts in Afghanistan and Iraq.

He began reading through radical Islamic websites and magazines that said the CIA staged the Sept. 11, 2001 terrorist attacks and that Jews control the world.

Some of the literature in the al Qaeda-backed magazine Inspire talked about how to build bombs.

Misha, who the FBI says has no terrorist ties, came to the Tsarnaev home to chat with Tamerlan about Islam. The chats worried Tamerlan's father, who was concerned about changes he saw in his eldest son.

A neighbor recalled after the marathon bombings that Tamerlan once called the Bible a "cheap copy" of the Koran.

Misha has since denied to the FBI and in news media reports that he influenced Tamerlan to become a radical Muslim.

One thing that did not change about Tamerlan was his hope of being an Olympic boxer.

He first mentioned it as a possibility after he won his first boxing matches in the United States as an 18-year-old.

The 2010 article in The Comment mentioned his dream under the headline, "Will Box for Passport."

The subhead said, "An Olympic Drive to Become a United States Citizen."

Tamerlan was quoted saying he hoped to win enough fights

to be chosen for the U.S. Olympic team. He said he would prefer to box for the United States rather than his native Russia, unless Chechnya gains independence.

But the pieces never seemed to fall in place for Tamerlan to make it onto the U.S. Olympic team. Moreover, his health became an issue, according to acquaintances.

His hopes of Olympic glory withered as he faced back problems and tough competitors.

He boxed in the 201-pound weight class of a Golden Gloves national championship tournament in Salt Lake City in May 2009. He lost in a first-round decision.

Edwin Rodriguez, a professional boxer in the super middleweight division, sparred with Tsarnaev in a Boston-area gym in 2010 on the recommendation of a friend.

"He had a little bit of a swagger to him, a real cocky kind of attitude," Rodriguez told Yahoo Sports.

Tamerlan punched hard but did not have the athletic finesse of a professional boxer, according to boxers who trained with him.

Rodriguez said Tamerlan complained about stomach pain after getting hit with a body punch. He also neglected to wear a mouth guard for the sparring session.

"He was bleeding from the mouth, which is pretty common if you're not wearing a mouth guard," Rodriguez told Yahoo Sports. "It's easy to get cut and he was spitting out blood and was complaining about pain in his stomach."

Rodriguez said he then went easier on him for the rest of the sparring session after seeing that Tamerlan was hurt.

Boxing coach John Curran, who trained both Rodriguez and Tamerlan, expressed amazement that he might be involved in a terrorist bombing.

"If I was asked two days before the bombing what I thought of this young man, I would have said he was a fine young man," Curran told ABC News. "Very good athlete. Very courteous, quiet and just a nice guy. I'm shocked beyond belief that he's involved, or that he was involved, in this."

A rule change for Golden Gloves boxers in 2010 forbade anyone who was not a U.S. citizen from fighting in the league, thereby ending Tamerlan's career.

As his boxing aspirations faltered, Islam remained his top priority.

Three-and-a-half years before the 2013 marathon bombings, Tamerlan married his new girlfriend on June 21, 2010 in a 15-minute ceremony at Masjid Al Quran mosque in the Boston suburb of Dorchester.

His wife was pregnant during the marriage ceremony. They had a daughter a few months later.

Tamerlan's devotion to Islam became a significant feature of his marriage.

He convinced his wife to convert to Islam and change her name to Karima Tsarnaev. Her maiden name was Katherine Russell. She began wearing a traditional Muslim head covering for women called a hijab.

Tamerlan grew a beard in the style suggested by the Koran. He shaved it shortly before the bombings. In the months leading up to the blasts, his wife supported the young family through her earnings as a home health aide, sometimes working as much as 70 hours per week.

Tamerlan remained largely unemployed. He stayed home to take care of the couple's young daughter.

His young wife later told the FBI she had no idea of her husband's involvement with terrorist activities.

In late 2010, Tamerlan's tendency to extrapolate his devotion to Islam into politics first came to the attention of the Federal Bureau of Investigation.

Russian security forces arrested a Muslim insurgent in December 2010 in Dagestan who disclosed his social network in the Islamic community, some of which was in North America.

One of the names he mentioned was Tamerlan Tsarnaev.

The Russian Federal Security Service notified the FBI about Tamerlan's radical Islamic tendencies in early 2011. They also claimed Tamerlan planned to join violent dissident groups in Russia.

The FBI later released a statement saying the Russian police warned them "that he had changed drastically since 2010 as he prepared to leave the United States for travel to the country's [Chechnya] region to join unspecified underground groups."

In response, FBI agents interviewed Tamerlan and his relatives. They also checked through government databases, telephone records of the Tsarnaevs, their travel history and their visits to Internet sites to search for links to radical Islam. They concluded that they could prove nothing suspicious.

An FBI spokesman described the interview of Tamerlan as a sit-down visit that turned up nothing unusual or threatening.

An FBI statement said the Russian police had told them Tamerlan "was a follower of radical Islam and a strong believer."

The FBI asked the Federal Security Service for more information following the interview with Tamerlan. After receiving no response, they closed the case.

The Russian Federal Security Service, along with the Central Intelligence Agency, continued to keep files on Tamerlan and his family. The CIA put Tamerlan and his mother on its Terrorist Identities Datamart Environment database after finding evidence Tamerlan once sent a text message to his mother in which he said he was ready to die for Islam.

In January 2012, Tamerlan returned to his native Russia for a visit with family, friends and fellow Muslims.

By the time he returned to the United States six months later, few people who knew him held lingering doubts about whether he might have turned to radical Islam.

Tamerlan traveled to the Dagestan region in Russia while he considered moving his young family to his boyhood home. His wife was interested in the opportunity to immerse herself in a different language and culture.

She stayed behind in Massachusetts while Tamerlan visited his parents. He also visited the hotbed of extremist Islam ideology in the North Caucuses, where separatists sometimes coupled their theology with violence.

Part of the trip consisted of innocent visits with his father to the homes of relatives. He helped his father renovate the family apartment in Makhachkala, where neighbors said he kept a low profile. Tamerlan also applied for a Russian passport.

U.S. investigators of the marathon bombings later unearthed what they believed was suspicious behavior by Tamerlan while he was in Russia, which they brought to the attention of Congress. U.S. House Homeland Security Chairman Michael McCaul said he wanted further investigation of whether Tamerlan received military-style training, which might have made him even more radical than his earlier behavior in the Boston area.

Evidence of any such training has been difficult to prove.

However, it is known that Tamerlan had extensive contact with a third cousin of his named Magomed Kartashov, a leader of an Islamist organization called the Union of the Just. The advocacy group believes Islam and its principles of sharia law should guide political systems. The group was outspoken in its criticisms of the United States.

Tamerlan sometimes talked about global "holy war" of Muslims against their perceived enemies, such as the United States, Great Britain and Israel, according to statements Kartashov made during interviews with Russia's Federal Security Service.

Dagestan police who track extremists reported Tamerlan made six visits to a mosque in his parents' hometown of Makhachkala frequented by Islamic militants.

Among the militants he was known to befriend were 23-year-old William Plotnikov and 19-year-old Makhmud Mansur Nidal.

Both of them were under surveillance by Russian police.

Before Tamerlan returned to the United States, both of them were killed by police in separate incidents. Plotnikov, a Russian-Canadian, already knew Tamerlan from when they both lived in the United States and trained as boxers. Plotnikov was one of six people killed in a July 2012 firefight with Russian forces in Dagestan.

The Russian newspaper Novaya Gazeta reported that Tamerlan tried to join Plotnikov's insurgency group in Dagestan. The group had "quarantined" Tamerlan for several months to verify his loyalty to their cause and to rule out risks he might be a double agent.

Two days after Plotnikov was killed, Tamerlan returned to Massachusetts suddenly. He did not even pick up his passport, which was one of the main reasons he traveled to Russia.

Russian police considered his hasty departure suspicious. His father insisted it was merely to complete his application for U.S. citizenship.

When he arrived in the United States on July 17, 2012, Tamerlan had grown a long, thick beard.

A neighbor of Tamerlan recalled seeing him in a Cambridge pizzeria after his return to the United States. He wore a light-colored turban, a checkered scarf and still sported the thick beard.

The neighbor described to The Wall Street Journal a good-natured argument he had with Tamerlan at the pizzeria.

"I kinda got the vibe that he was idolizing the Koran and trash talking, or talking down, the Christian Bible," the neighbor said. "He said that the Bible was used as an excuse to invade other countries."

Tamerlan said the United States was a colonial power trying to seize control in the Middle East, the neighbor said.

"He mentioned how in the wars in Afghanistan and Iraq most casualties are innocent people gunned down by American soldiers," the neighbor said.

The argument ended with the two of them resolving their differences enough to shake hands.

About the same time, Tamerlan posted video on YouTube that showed Islamists who advocated "jihad," or holy war, against the West.

One of the videos featured Gadzhimurad Dolgatov, a commander of a small insurgent group in Dagestan. He was killed by the Russian military in December 2012, only months after taking the helm of his band of violent dissidents.

The Russian-language video shows Dolgatov quoting the Koran from memory and encouraging young Muslims to join the jihad. Around him are gun-carrying masked men.

"If you think Islam can be spread without spilling a single drop of blood, you're wrong," Dolgatov said in the video. He also said "only cowards and hypocrites seek excuses not to join the jihad."

Commentators on other Islamist websites called Dolgatov a "martyr" and a "brave lion of Allah."

By itself the video is similar to the kind commonly found among Islamic insurgents. Even more interesting to the FBI was how and why Tamerlan Tsarnaev gained access to it and posted it on YouTube.

They theorized that the video showed a high degree of awareness of terrorist groups in the North Caucausus region, which is one of the places Tamerlan visited during his 2012 visit to Russia.

Tamerlan put a link on his YouTube account to another video that showed the radical cleric Feiz Mohammad. Voices can be heard singing on the video while bombs explode.

On September 5, 2012, Tamerlan applied for U.S. citizenship.

However, a routine review of law enforcement records by immigration officials showed that Tamerlan was interviewed by the FBI in January 2011 on request of the Russian government.

Rather than following routine procedures, immigration officials decided to delay Tamerlan's application for citizenship for what they called additional review.

Tamerlan's fellow Muslims at the mosque he attended in Cambridge started having misgivings about his zealousness to Islam.

During one sermon in November 2012, Tamerlan stood up to challenge the speaker after he said that in the same way "we all celebrate the birthday of the Prophet, we can also celebrate July 4 and Thanksgiving."

Tamerlan responded that he "took offense to celebrating anything," according to a spokesman for the mosque.

Then in January 2013 — three months before the marathon bombings — Tamerlan interrupted a Martin Luther King, Jr. Day sermon at the mosque.

In a loud voice, he complained that he objected to the speaker's comparison of Martin Luther King, Jr. with the Prophet Mohammed.

Other members of the congregation shouted him down. He was told not to return to the mosque unless he could refrain from interrupting and shouting during the sermons.

For the next three months, Tamerlan seemed to drop out of sight — until he and his brother's images appeared on video near the finish line of the Boston Marathon.

DZHOKHAR TSARNAEV

UNTIL DZHOKHAR ANZOROVICH Tsarnaev burst into the spotlight in April 2013, he fell into a nondescript void where most college students dwell.

He was born July 22, 1993 in the mountainous Russian republic of Kyrgyzstan.

His parents brought 8-year-old Dzhokhar with them to the United States while Tamerlan and the two daughters, Ailina and Bella, stayed behind with relatives. They joined their parents at their rented three-bedroom house at 410 Norfolk Street in Cambridge in July 2003, when Tamerlan was 15 years old. Tamerlan and Dzhokhar shared a bedroom with a bunk bed. The two daughters shared a second bedroom.

The family was granted permanent residency by the U.S. government in March 2007 under political asylum regulations of immigration law.

By that time, Dzhokhar had started attending high school at Cambridge Rindge and Latin School. The students included the children of professors from nearby Harvard University and the Massachusetts Institute of Technology, who often would continue their educations at equally prestigious colleges.

Famous alumni of the school included the actors Ben Affleck and Matt Damon.

Another large portion of the student body came from working class families that sometimes dipped into food stamps and welfare for support, similar to the Tsarnaev family. Others lived in public housing. About 50 nationalities are represented among the school's students.

The high school, whose name commonly was shortened to Rindge, was known for its tolerance of ethnic diversity and alternate lifestyles.

"It's a very multicultural place and we're proud of that," Peter Payack, Dzhokhar's wrestling coach, said in an interview for this report. "We see good things in a lot of different people."

Even Dzhokhar's Muslim heritage, which would have branded him as a troublemaker in many other schools and communities, was met with easy acceptance at Rindge.

"It's not like he was the only Muslim. We have a lot of Muslims," Payack said. "He was just like the guy who was from the Dominican Republic, from China, from Ireland."

Once, during his high school wrestling days, Payack asked Dzhokhar about his religious affiliation.

"I asked him, 'Are you a Muslim,'" Payack said. "He said, 'Yeah, I'm a Muslim but I'm not really a Muslim.'"

Payack interpreted Dzhokhar's response to mean he was nonchalant in his approach to his native religion, certainly not the radical he appeared to be later.

Dzhokhar was generally a good student who was known for skateboarding, wrestling and his preference for rap music. He spoke English with only a trace of a foreign accent.

Few of his friends or acquaintances could pronounce his name with the Russian flair it required. With the help of Payack, Dzhokhar took on the nickname of the more easily pronounced Jahar. Others who had trouble with Jahar called him Joe.

"It was the only name we could pronounce," Payack said. "I

said how about Jahar and he said yeah, and we laughed and that became it."

He drew a circle of friends who never would have guessed Dzhokhar was anything other than a likeable classmate. A senior prom photo shows him wearing a black tuxedo with a red bow tie in a group shot of his fellow high school students.

His extracurricular interest in wrestling led him to become captain of his high school wrestling team in his junior year and a Greater Boston League Winter All-Star. He sometimes trained in boxing with his older brother at his local gym.

Payack remembered him as much for his intelligence as his wrestling skill. Dzhokhar was nominated to the National Honor Society during his sophomore year. The coach also remembered him for his even, calm temperament that allowed him to fit in easily with classmates and teammates.

Although he could have used his wrestling and boxing skills to hurt a rival, Dzhokhar showed no desire to do so.

"He was our captain, which meant that not only was he a good wrestler, he was a respected wrestler," Payack said. "It was somebody we put a lot of faith and trust in."

Payack had no idea that after he graduated his respected wrestler was changing. "Apparently he fell under his brother's influence," Payack said.

Even then, nothing obvious about his behavior aroused suspicions of deep trouble brewing.

Dzhokhar earned money after school as a lifeguard at nearby Harvard University's Malkin Athletic Center pool, only a few blocks from his high school. His coworkers remembered him as friendly and dutifully attending to his job assignments.

He never publicly displayed the kind of vociferous loyalty to Islam like his older brother. He sometimes drank alcohol, according to high school friends.

Dzhokhar's only hint of strong political feelings came on the rare occasions he talked about what the Russians were doing to

Chechens. One fellow lifeguard said only then would Dzhokhar show feelings of "hatred" and "anger," all of it directed at the Russians.

After he graduated in 2011, Dzhokhar won a $2,500 college scholarship from the City of Cambridge. Only about 40 students a year won the scholarships.

He considered going to a better college, like Tufts, but was concerned about the high costs and risks that it might financially burden his struggling parents.

He enrolled at the University of Massachusetts at Dartmouth, majoring in marine biology. He planned first to become an engineer but then seemed to change his mind by saying he wanted to be a dentist.

Like his brother, Dzhokhar struggled in college to balance his unstable finances with the need to be diligent in his studies. His college transcript showed he received seven failing grades over three semesters.

They included F's in Chemistry and the Environment, Principles of Modern Chemistry and Introduction to American Politics. He received a B in Critical Writing.

Shortly after arriving at college, Dzhokhar dropped hints that he would prefer to be at home. The university, like the city of North Dartmouth, had little spark or excitement to offer the young immigrant. The university sits in a blue-collar community that has a plethora of fast food restaurants as one of its most striking features.

Like in high school, none of his college classmates noticed anything unusual about Dzhokhar. He lived in a dorm, played intramural soccer, worked out in the college gym and wore jeans, T-shirts and sweaters.

His friends said Dzhokhar not only smoked, but also occasionally sold, marijuana.

Dzhokhar published a profile of himself on the Russian social networking site Vkontakte. He wrote that he spoke

English, Russian and the Chechen language Nohchiyn Mott. He listed his religion as Islam and claimed personal goals of "career and money."

He posted a joke with his profile that said, "There is a car... in the car sit a Dagestani, a Chechen and an Ingush. Question — who is driving? The answer: The Police."

Dzhokhar often went home to Cambridge on weekends. But by his freshman year, home was becoming a different place.

His sisters had left in what were believed to be arranged marriages. His parents had separated and his father returned to Russia.

Anzor suffered from headaches, stomach pain and arthritis. He blamed part of his health problems on beatings he suffered in Kyrgyzstan that he said were prompted by ethnic hatred.

In Cambridge, he also found that his work as an auto mechanic could not support his family, forcing them to go back onto public assistance after five years. His neighbors reported seeing an uneven temperament in Anzor, sometimes laughing loudly, other times arguing with them over parking spaces.

Anzor tried to work hard but never reached the wealth he hoped to attain in America. Increasingly, the family turned to Zubeidat's earnings as a cosmetologist. After first working in a local salon, she started her own business in her home.

Like her son Tamerlan, Zubeidat also was known for being a devout Muslim. Anzor, however, never took more than a passing interest in Islam.

He moved back to Russia in 2011 and was granted a divorce shortly afterward. At that point, the family seemed to splinter, according to friends and neighbors.

Zubeidat was arrested for trying to steal $1,600 worth of clothes from a Lord & Taylor clothing store in the United States. While she was out of jail on bond, she returned to Russia to avoid prosecution. There, she reconciled with her husband.

Dzhokhar's two sisters were living in New Jersey after

apparently abandoning their young marriages.

When Dzhokhar went home from college to Cambridge, the only family member to meet him was his brother Tamerlan. The advice Tamerlan gave to him included telling him to pray five times per day to thank Allah.

In fact, Tamerlan — always a guiding figure for the Tsarnaev children — was taking on a bigger role in his kid brother's life.

He started taking him to Friday prayers at their local mosque. Tamerlan's former boxing coach described Dzhokhar as being like his older brother's "puppy dog" for the way he would follow him around.

Dzhokhar's shift toward a more straight-laced Muslim frame of mind shows in the Tweets he would send friends and that were retrieved by Rolling Stone for a magazine article.

In November 2011, only months after arriving at Dartmouth, he sent a Tweet that could have come from any college freshman when he wrote, "Using my high school essays for my English class #its that easy. You know what i like to do? Answer my own questions cuz no one else can."

His homesickness showed in a June 2012 Tweet when he wrote, "I can see my face in my dad's pictures as a youngin, he even had a ridiculous amount of hair like me."

By that time, home for him meant that he lived with his older brother and his sister-in-law.

In a March 2012 Twitter message, he wrote, "A decade in America already. I want out."

He still showed the good-natured attitude that brought him friends. While lifeguarding at the Harvard pool during summer break from college, he tweeted, "I didn't become a lifeguard to just chill and get paid. I do it for the people, saving lives brings me joy."

By August 2012, when he left the home of Tamerlan's family to return to college, he was starting to show signs of political disenchantment.

Referring to the $15 billion spent on the Summer Olympics, he tweeted, "Imagine if that money was used to feed those in need all over the world. The value of human life ain't shit nowadays that's #tragic."

In another Tweet, he wrote, "Idk why it's hard for many of you to accept that 9/11 was an inside job, I mean I guess fuck the facts y'all are some real #patriots #gethip."

Ironically, on September 11, 2012, Dzhokhar gained the American citizenship he sought.

While home for Christmas break in 2012, and continuing to delve deeper into Islam, Dzhokhar tweeted, "I meet the most amazing people. My religion is the truth."

In a January 15, 2013 Tweet, he wrote, "I don't argue with fools who say Islam is terrorism it's not worth a thing, let an idiot remain an idiot."

In a March 18 Tweet, he wrote, "People come into your life to help you, hurt you, love you and leave you and that shapes your character and the person you were meant to be. Evil triumphs when good men do nothing."

On April 7, he tweeted, "If you have the knowledge and the inspiration all that's left is to take action."

On April 11, Dzhohkhar sent a Tweet saying, "Most of you are conditioned by the media."

On the evening of April 14, Dzhokhar skateboarded down Norfolk Street near his family's home in Cambridge. A neighbor called out a greeting and commended him on his skateboard. Neighbors recall Dzhokhar responded with something like "Yeah, thanks."

On April 15, the homemade bombs exploded at the Boston Marathon.

THE CHASE IS ON

NOTHING ABOUT THE Tsarnaev brothers' behavior after April 15 gave a hint of involvement in the bombings.

Tamerlan returned to his family home in Cambridge to take care of his 3-year-old daughter while his wife worked.

Police later found a time-dated grocery store receipt showing Dzhokhar went shopping at Whole Foods in Cambridge hours after the bombings.

Also on Monday, Dzhokhar tweeted his friends with the message, "Ain't no love in the heart of the city. Stay safe people."

Later that day, he sent another Tweet saying, "There are people that know the truth but stay silent & there are people that speak the truth but we don't hear them cuz they're the minority."

On Tuesday afternoon, Dzhokhar went to Junior Auto Body shop near his family's home in Cambridge to pick up a Mercedes-Benz he left there two weeks earlier. He said the car belonged to a girlfriend.

The rear bumper was not yet repaired, but Dzhokhar told the auto mechanic, Gilberto Junior, he wanted the car anyway.

"I need it now," Dzhokhar reportedly told Junior.

Junior described Dzhokhar as acting unusually nervous,

biting his fingernails, his knees shaking, almost as though he had been on drugs.

By Tuesday afternoon, Dzhokhar's security card swipes showed that he had returned to his single-unit dorm at the University of Massachusetts at Dartmouth's Pine Dale Hall.

He worked out in the weight room at the campus fitness center, where he was spotted on a security camera, and slept in his dorm that night.

He tweeted his friends to describe as "fake" a story about a woman killed during the marathon bombings who was found dead by her boyfriend shortly before he planned to propose marriage to her. He even joked about dreaming of eating a cheeseburger but instead getting a hot dog.

On Wednesday, April 17, Dzhokhar attended a soccer party at his college. Most partygoers described him as acting relaxed and no different than any other time.

He sent a Tweet that night with lyrics from the rapper Eminem saying, "Nowadays everybody wanna talk like they got something to say but nothing comes out when they move their lips; just a bunch of gibberish."

Just after midnight, he sent another Tweet to his friends saying, "I'm a stress-free kind of guy."

The next day around 5 p.m., the FBI released photos of two young men they called "Suspect 1" and "Suspect 2." The photos were broadcast on television screens throughout the United States and internationally.

The two brothers' photos and personal information already were in government databases, such as federal immigration records and the Massachusetts Registry of Motor Vehicles.

But the photos and video from the marathon were too grainy for the FBI's face-recognition technology to match them to government records. In addition, Tamerlan wore sunglasses and the images were taken at side angles from their faces.

The photos that appeared on television screens, including

the ones at Dartmouth and in the Cambridge neighborhood that included the Tsarnaev family home, were good enough for acquaintances to recognize the Tsarnaevs.

Tamerlan and Dzhokhar suddenly disappeared from their friends, family and anyone else who knew them.

They are accused of developing a terrorist plot that slipped through a sophisticated detection web of the Massachusetts State Police, the FBI and the CIA. However, they had no effective plan for escaping once they were identified.

"These guys did not have an exit plan after the bombing, and from the way they have both ended up, it looks like they planned on never being taken alive," a law enforcement source later told the local news media.

Less than a day after the FBI published the photos on television, another false story about a suspect ran through the local community and media. The reports said a suspect had been arrested and was headed to the federal courthouse in Boston.

Hundreds of reporters flocked to the courthouse in South Boston while the Coast Guard and police patrolled the river nearby with machine guns on their boats. At the Moakley courthouse, staff members expressed concern they would need a bigger courtroom than the one normally used by the emergency magistrate.

The fervor was quieted only after the FBI issued a statement saying there was no arrest.

By then, the chaos included a bomb threat received by the building's management company. The U.S. Marshals Service ordered the federal courthouse evacuated about 3 p.m.

A crowd of courthouse staff, journalists and gawkers gathered outside the building as a bomb squad first searched it then gave it an "all clear."

Meanwhile, the Tsarnaev brothers were making a desperate effort to escape, according to police. Later evidence indicated they hoped to disappear somewhere into the masses of New

York City, where Times Square beckoned as their next possible bombing target.

But with a half-baked escape plan, they had to figure out some way fast of getting the money, the weapons and the means of travel they needed to elude capture. Dzhokhar's green Honda Civic would be identified quickly by police, ruling it out as a getaway car. Their only weapons consisted of a handgun and a BB gun.

One of their first priorities was to get more firepower, which led them to a deadly run-in with a 27-year-old police officer named Sean A. Collier, who worked at the Massachusetts Institute of Technology.

A NIGHT OF GUNS

ONE OF THE notable characteristics of Sean Collier's job at MIT was what some police officers would call a lack of excitement.

There were doors to check, occasional car wrecks, a few drunks to roust, but only rarely the kind of violence that keeps police in Chicago, Los Angeles or New York City hopping.

A big part of the reason was MIT. Some academics regard it as America's most venerable college of science and engineering, a place where students and faculty come as a step toward leading roles in organizations like Apple Inc., Microsoft Corp. or the National Aeronautics and Space Administration.

Few of them are interested in sidetracking their careers by risking criminal convictions.

Collier wanted more to his career than the relatively complacent life of a campus cop. He had worked for the MIT Police Department for only 15 months. He sought a new job with the nearby Somerville Police Department, which was near his hometown of Wilmington and offered a more traditional police officer's lifestyle.

His five siblings said Collier wanted to be a police officer since he was 7 years old. "He was born to be a police officer and he lived his dreams," according to his brother, Rob Rogers. His supervisors gave him high marks for balancing his law enforcement duties along with friendly relations with the local community.

He was known as a fan of country music and a clumsy but dedicated square dancer.

When Collier told his colleagues about his application to the Somerville Police Department, his supervisors assured him he could leave on good terms.

But if complacency was an issue in his MIT job, it all ended abruptly on the evening of April 18, 2013.

Collier was parked in his car near Kendall Square in Cambridge to watch for motorists who sometimes took illegal shortcuts through campus to avoid traffic lights. The MIT Police chief pulled up beside him to chat momentarily then drove away. Collier's 3 p.m. to 11:15 p.m. shift was nearing its end.

A security camera tells the rest of the story.

Two young men approached Collier's car from the rear around 10:30 p.m. The larger of the two men, allegedly Tamerlan Tsarnaev, raised a gun. Without conversation, he fired into the seated police officer five times.

All five of the shots hit Collier, two of them in the head. Investigators said the execution-style murder gave the police officer no time to protect himself.

After Collier slumped in his seat, one of the brothers allegedly opened his car door. Dzhokhar is accused of trying to steal Collier's service gun from his holster. However, the MIT police use retention holsters that lock the guns in place.

The suspects were unable to remove Collier's gun from the holster. After struggling unsuccessfully to steal the gun, they walked away.

The April 23 memorial for the young police officer brought about 10,000 mourners to MIT's athletic field. Many wore police uniforms, some were students familiar with Collier and others were members of the community who never met him.

"It is so difficult to understand why such a senseless, brutal act was perpetrated on such a gentle, caring young man," MIT Police Chief John DiFava said during the memorial service.

Folk singer and Massachusetts native James Taylor sang at the Briggs Field service. Vice President Joseph Biden delivered one of the eulogies.

He spoke about his own experience of losing a child while commending Collier's "incredible family" and deploring the terrorism that brought mourners to the service.

"Why, whether it's Al Qaeda, or two twisted, perverted, cowardly knockoff jihadis here in Boston, why do they do what they do?" Biden asked.

"They do it to instill fear," he said. Later, he added, "We have suffered, we are grieving, but we are not bending."

The shooting did not end Collier's career as a police officer. Four months later, the Somerville Police Department posthumously appointed him as one of their own officers.

The shooting also was not the last gunplay for the evening of April 18. In fact, it was only beginning.

As police converged on the MIT campus, a 26-year-old Chinese immigrant and entrepreneur who, before his real name was revealed at Dzhokhar's trial, used only his nickname of Danny to protect his privacy, pulled to the curb in Boston's Brighton/Allston neighborhood to answer a text message.

A Honda Civic sedan swerved to a slamming stop behind his new Mercedes SUV. A man in dark clothes got out and approached on the passenger side of the black Mercedes.

The man knocked on the window and said something quickly that Danny could not understand. Danny lowered the window, prompting the unknown man to reach in, unlock the door and climb in.

"Don't be stupid," the man said as he aimed a silver handgun toward Danny, according to a Boston Globe report.

The man, later identified as Tamerlan Tsarnaev, asked Danny whether he had heard of the bombings at the Boston Marathon. When Danny said yes, Tamerlan told him, "I did that."

Then he added, "And I just killed a policeman in Cambridge."

Danny was the only witness who could verify Tamerlan's words in an extensive interview he gave the Boston Globe. He said Tamerlan then ordered him to drive, telling him where to turn in a meandering 75-minute trip through Brighton, Watertown and back to Cambridge. Danny did as he was told while he secretly worried that his life might end suddenly and soon.

Dzhokhar followed behind them in the Tsarnaev brothers' Honda Civic sedan.

"Don't look at me," Tamerlan shouted to him as Danny glanced toward his abductor. "Do you remember my face?"

"No, no, I don't remember anything," Danny responded in his Chinese accent.

At another point, Tamerlan laughed and said, "It's like white guys. They look at black guys and think all black guys look the same. And maybe you think all white guys look the same."

"Exactly," said Danny, despite the fact his well-educated engineering mind remembered everything about the Tsarnaev brothers and their abduction of him.

As the threat of sudden death made Danny nervous, he had difficulty staying in one lane. Tamerlan told him, "Relax."

Tamerlan remarked on Danny's Chinese ancestry by saying, "Okay, that's why your English is not very good. Okay, you're Chinese ... I'm a Muslim."

"Chinese are very friendly to Muslims," Danny said. "We are so friendly to Muslims."

While still concerned that robbery was their prime motive and trying to downplay his wealth, Danny told Tamerlan his new $50,000 Mercedes was older than it seemed and the lease payments were lower than the actual cost, according to the Boston Globe report.

When Tamerlan demanded money, Danny gave him the $45 in his armrest. He handed over his wallet but it contained only credit cards. Tamerlan pulled out an ATM card and asked Danny to tell him the PIN code.

As they traveled through Watertown, Tamerlan ordered him to pull over on a side street. Dzhokhar stopped the sedan behind them and walked to the SUV. Danny thought he recognized the shaggy-haired Dzhokhar from the images of two men the FBI introduced on television hours earlier as "Suspect 1" and "Suspect 2."

Tamerlan got out of the Mercedes and ordered Danny into the passenger seat. He warned him that he would shoot Danny if he caused problems.

Dzhokhar and Tamerlan spent several minutes loading heavy objects from the sedan into the trunk of the Mercedes SUV, which Danny thought looked like luggage.

Police investigation later would show the luggage was packed with explosives.

Tamerlan took over as the driver while Dzhokhar climbed into the backseat. Danny sat in the passenger seat of his own car as he contemplated how to escape, and whether he could make it away alive. The Tsarnaevs left their sedan parked along the side street curb.

The Tsarnaevs asked Danny about his credit limit. When he told them it was only $1,000, they acted as though they did not believe him.

Danny told them that his short time in the United States had not allowed him to build enough of a credit history for a bigger limit.

They then asked whether he had a girlfriend. When he told them his girlfriend was in China, they asked whether anyone cared about him. In an effort to make them believe they could gain nothing by killing him, Danny told them no.

Tamerlan drove to Watertown Square on Main Street, where

Dzhokhar got out to withdraw money from a Bank of America ATM with Danny's debit card. Danny shivered from fear but tried to hide it by saying he was cold. He asked to get his jacket from the back seat. Tamerlan agreed to get it for him.

While Dzhokhar was out of the car, Danny considered making a break for freedom but saw only closed stores around him at the strip mall that offered no chance of refuge. A police car drove by with its lights off. Danny decided an escape now would be too risky.

Danny unbuckled his seatbelt to put on his jacket. Afterward, he tried to slide the seatbelt buckle behind himself to prepare for a fast escape.

Tamerlan watched him and suspected Danny's motive for not putting his seatbelt back on.

"Don't do that," Tamerlan said. "Don't be stupid."

After Dzhokhar returned to the car, Tamerlan told Danny, "We both have guns." Danny did not see a second gun.

As they continued on their wayward trek, which included passing a police station, Tamerlan asked Danny to turn on his radio and demonstrate how it worked. Tamerlan ran through several radio stations before asking Danny whether he had any CDs. Danny said he had none because he preferred to listen to music on his phone.

As he noticed the fuel gauge dropping, Tamerlan pulled into a gas station, only to find the pumps were closed for the night. He turned around and headed back toward Watertown where he knew other gas stations would be open.

Tamerlan slid a CD into the vehicle's CD player that played instrumental Middle Eastern music. Danny thought it sounded like a call to prayer for Muslims.

Danny asked Tamerlan, "Are you going to hurt me?"

He replied, "I'm not going to hurt you. We're just going to drop you off ... Probably you'll have to walk four or five miles to find anybody, and if you are lucky, somebody will pick you up."

Danny told the Boston Globe that he prayed during the ordeal.

As the Middle Eastern music played, Danny's iPhone buzzed with a text message from his roommate. The roommate knew about the police killing at MIT and she was concerned about why he had not returned home by his usual time. The text message was written in Chinese.

Tamerlan demanded to know what the message said. He grabbed Danny's iPhone. He knew enough about software for iPhones that he asked Danny whether he had an app for translating between Chinese and English.

Danny said he did have the translation app. Tamerlan then used it to type in, "I'm sick, I'm sleeping at a friend's." He copied it and returned the message.

But the message only aroused more suspicions in the roommate, who sent another text message to inquire further. No one responded.

Her boyfriend called Danny on his iPhone at 12:03 a.m. As the phone rang, Tamerlan pointed the silver handgun at Danny.

"Answer it," Tamerlan said angrily. "If you say a single word in Chinese, I will kill you right now." He told Danny what he should say.

The caller spoke in Mandarin, saying, "Where are you?"

Danny answered back in English. "I'm sleeping in my friend's home tonight," he said. "I'm sorry, I have to go."

As the call ended, Tamerlan told him, "Good boy. Good job."

The Tsarnaev brothers spoke to each other in their native language, none of which Danny understood ... except for one word: "Manhattan." They asked him whether he could drive his car out of state.

"What do you mean," Danny asked.

"Like New York," one of the brothers said.

Only later would the FBI compile evidence the Tsarnaev brothers' next bomb target was Times Square in the heart of New York City.

The brothers' conversation began including occasional comments that showed their youth. They discussed girls, the iPhone 5, credit limits for students and whether anyone still listened to compact discs. They spoke admirably about the Mercedes ML 350 they had carjacked.

The fuel gauge on the SUV showed it could not wait much longer for gasoline. Tamerlan drove down Soldiers Field Road, passed Harvard Business School, turned left on a bridge in front of the Doubletree Hotel and then another left into the Shell Station on Memorial Drive to buy gas.

Tamerlan pulled the car up to the gas pumps on the right, next to Danny. Dzhokhar got out to fill up and to pay with Danny's credit card. He tapped on the car window moments later after seeing a sign that said the station accepted cash only.

Tamerlan handed Dzhokhar $50 in cash. As Dzhokhar walked toward the cashier to pay, Danny was alone in his car with Tamerlan.

"Maybe I have a chance," Danny thought. "It's my last chance to get out."

It was around 12:15 a.m., nearly an hour and a half since he was abducted. Danny realized it was a critical moment: The doors were unlocked. Dzhokhar was in the store.

"I was thinking I must do two things: unfasten my seatbelt and open the door and jump out as quick as I can. If I didn't make it, he would kill me right out, he would kill me right away," Danny told the Boston Globe.

Tamerlan put his gun in the door cubby on the left side while he used both hands to fiddle with a GPS navigation device he had brought with him. Danny saw his chance.

He visualized his own escape momentarily before flipping the seat belt buckle open with one hand while simultaneously grabbing the door handle with the other hand. He hopped out of the SUV as Tamerlan grabbed at his jacket and slammed the door behind him.

"Fuck," he heard Tamerlan shout.

He sprinted at an angle between the car and gas pumps to deprive Tamerlan of a clear shooting angle toward him. From that moment on, time was running out for the Tsarnaev brothers.

Danny ran to a nearby Mobil gas station across the street where he breathlessly shouted for the clerk to call 911. After brief confusion about details of the emergency, the clerk used a portable phone to call the police dispatcher then gave it to Danny. The dispatcher told Danny to take a deep breath as he hid in a storeroom.

Police cars arrived in less than five minutes. By that time, the Tsarnaev brothers had roared off in Danny's SUV toward Watertown. Danny told the officers his iPhone and an anti-theft tracking device in his Mercedes should allow them to find the suspects. Police tried tracking the vehicle with the tracking device and received a "ping" telling them the location of the SUV.

Tamerlan would be dead in about one hour.

END OF THE ROAD FOR THE TSARNAEVS

THE TSARNAEVS HEADED back toward Cambridge to retrieve their parked Honda Civic as police dispatchers put out an alert to all patrol cars in the Watertown and Cambridge areas to watch for the now stolen Mercedes SUV.

Minutes later, police tracked the Tsarnaevs driving through Watertown.

As the first Watertown police car spotted them and did a U-turn to pull in behind them, the Tsarnaevs drove down Dexter Avenue and made a left turn onto Laurel Street before pulling to the side of the road. Dzhokhar drove the Honda Civic while Tamerlan drove the SUV.

The brothers got out and took up positions behind the Mercedes while facing the police car. As the first police car approached, Tamerlan started walking toward the cruiser and shooting at it. The police officer driving the vehicle halted and jammed his car in reverse to put about 30 yards more distance between him and the shooter. Tamerlan returned to cover behind the Mercedes.

More police cars arrived, again drawing fire from Tamerlan.

One of the officers ducked down as bullets hit his windshield.

One of the bullets "went right by his ear and landed in the headrest," Lieutenant Michael Lawn of the Watertown Police Department said for this report.

The officer put the transmission of his stopped car in drive and climbed out a door to let the police cruiser proceed without passengers toward the Tsarnaevs.

He was trying to draw their fire so they would waste ammunition, which is precisely what Tamerlan did, peppering the empty car with several bullets. The driverless car stopped after hitting two cars in a driveway.

The next five minutes were filled with only barely controlled back and forth gunfire. The Tsarnaevs reportedly threw five crude homemade hand grenades at the police, three of which exploded but injured no one.

During the firefight, transit police officer Richard H. Donohue was shot in the upper right leg near his groin, possibly by one of his colleagues who had aimed poorly.

He later was taken to a nearby hospital in critical condition. A trauma team gave him a transfusion and did CPR on him until his blood pressure rose to normal levels. He was put in intensive care on a ventilator.

Before Donohue was retrieved by an ambulance, both Tamerlan and Dzhokhar were wounded by police bullets. Tamerlan was hit nine times.

Tamerlan walked out into the open toward the officers firing his gun at them and carrying a bulky object. Police identified it as the same kind of pressure-cooker bomb detonated at the Boston Marathon.

He lit the bomb and threw it at the officers. However, the lid dislodged and Tamerlan was able to throw it only about 20 yards, not close enough to the police to hurt them. Nevertheless, the bomb exploded, making a big bang and sending a burst of light cascading through the neighborhood.

Tamerlan started walking toward one of the officers closest to him while shooting his gun at him.

"He all of a sudden comes out from under cover and just starts walking down the street, shooting at our police officers, trying to get closer," Watertown Police Chief Edward Deveau later told the media.

Tamerlan's gun suddenly stopped firing. He looked at the gun, realized he was out of ammunition and threw it at the officer he had just tried to kill. The gun hit the police officer in the left bicep as Tamerlan turned to run toward the street. The police officer ran after him.

"One sergeant tackled him," Lawn said. "The other sergeant was fearful that he had more explosives on him and that's why he was coming at them."

A quick search of the now seriously wounded Tamerlan showed no vests packed with explosives as the officers feared. While three officers handcuffed Tamerlan, Dzhokhar jumped back into the damaged Mercedes and drove it toward the officers.

The next few seconds remain clouded by differing reports. Police said that as their officers jumped out of the way, Dzhokhar ran over his own brother, dragging him under the SUV for about 20 feet. An eyewitness said Tamerlan was struck by a police SUV before officers shot him multiple times.

Shortly after he was wheeled into Beth Israel Deaconess Medical Center unconscious on a gurney under heavy police guard, he went into cardiac arrest. Emergency room personnel tried to revive him for about 10 minutes.

As police officers looked on, the trauma doctors and nurses did CPR on Tamerlan. They put a breathing tube down his throat. They cut open his chest to see whether blood was collecting around his heart.

They asked police to remove his handcuffs so they could move him around more easily. The trauma team was unable to get Tamerlan's heart beating again. They pronounced him dead at 1:35 a.m.

Emergency room doctors described Tamerlan's injuries as massive blood loss, cardiac arrest and respiratory arrest. They did not initally realize he had been run over by a vehicle.

His death certificate from the Massachusetts Office of the Chief Medical Examiner lists his cause of death as gunshot wounds to the torso and extremities along with blunt trauma to the head and torso. The certificate says he was hit and dragged by a vehicle.

An autopsy photograph leaked to the media showed multiple gunshot wounds, a gash running from the center of his chest to his back and a smaller gash below it. His right shoulder and face show obvious hemorrhaging, some of which could have been inflicted by hospital staff members while trying to revive him.

Dzhokhar had sped away from the scene of the shootout in the stolen SUV. By that time, a police helicopter was taking up a position overhead. Residents said they heard and saw the black SUV careen over a slight hill and slam to a stop about a half-mile away from where Tamerlan lay critically injured. The front end was bent, one headlight out and the passenger side of the windshield damaged by police bullets.

Police later recovered about 200 rounds of spent gun shells from the scene of the shooting, the 9 millimeter semi-automatic handgun Tamerlan shot at them and a BB gun apparently dropped by Dzhokhar. Most of the shots fired flew wide of their marks, including some into the homes of neighborhood residents.

Police chased after Dzhokhar. The first patrol car arrived at the spot where Dzhokhar abandoned the SUV with its red lights flashing and siren blaring about 45 seconds after it halted abruptly on a residential street. Police officers approached the vehicle slowly, cautiously, with guns drawn.

But by that time, Dzhokhar had run off and disappeared between houses in a neighborhood he had seen previously. He smashed and broke his cellphone so it could not be tracked.

The police rushed to surround and cordon off the entire neighborhood to prevent Dzhokhar from escaping. At the request of the Massachusetts governor, they put out bulletins on local radio and television stations asking all residents of Boston, Belmont, Cambridge, Newton, Waltham and Watertown to stay inside their homes. They shut down public transportation at 6 a.m. Some residents were escorted from their own homes by police who had their guns drawn.

Shutting down all access to a 20-block area in Watertown caused a delay in the chase as police SWAT teams arrived and more patrol cars took up positions in the neighborhood.

It also gave people who knew Dzhokhar an opportunity to make a plea to him on the chance he might be watching television.

His uncle, Ruslan Tsarni, said on live television the next day, "Dzhokhar, if you are alive, turn yourself in and ask for forgiveness." He said Dzhokhar had shamed his family and Chechens.

His high school wrestling coach realized for the first time early in the morning on April 19 that the man in the surveillance images of the FBI's "Suspect 2" was Dzhokhar.

"When I got the phone call [from a fellow coach], I felt like my heart exploded," Payack said. "It was somebody I not only knew, I liked. I was shocked beyond belief."

An FBI agent who had discovered the mutual respect between Dzhokhar and his coach asked Payack to appeal to the now-wanted fugitive to turn himself in to the police. "I felt it was my responsibility," Payack said.

Ironically, Payack — a veteran runner of 12 Boston marathons — was one of the injured from the April 15 bombings. He had been close enough to the finish line that the first blast damaged his inner ear and hearing. He had difficulty sleeping in the next four days.

He spoke with CNN the afternoon of April 19. During the

interview he issued a plea to Dzhokhar.

"Jahar," he said while invoking his nickname. "This is Coach Payack. There has been enough death, destruction. Please turn yourself in."

Thousands of police were searching door-to-door and backyard-to-backyard in the small suburban town of Watertown. Residents were reminded again to stay indoors as a crowd of onlookers grew outside the police line surrounding the community.

The college freshman had pulled back a tie-down line on a tarpaulin over a 22-foot motorboat in a resident's backyard, about a quarter-mile from where he abandoned the SUV. He crawled inside, apparently hoping to wait out the police manhunt while he lay bleeding from a gunshot wound.

Instead, on the evening of April 19, the boat owner, David Henneberry, noticed the tarp over his boat appeared to be dislodged on one corner and was flapping in the wind. He told his stepson that perhaps a squirrel had forced its way into the boat.

When the Massachusetts governor lifted the order at 6 p.m. for residents of the Watertown neighborhood to stay inside their homes, or "shelter in place," Henneberry went outside to check on his boat.

He noticed the tie-down strap was looser than normal. He adjusted it and returned to his white clapboard house. But he had an uneasy feeling something still was wrong with his boat, called the Slip Away.

He went back outside, got a stepladder and put it against his boat. Three steps up the ladder, he lifted the tarpaulin, pulled back the shrink-wrap and looked inside. He saw blood on the floor of the boat, a lot of it.

As he looked toward the engine block, the darkness created by the boat's cover allowed him to see only the contours of a slim man's body crumpled up in a ball in the bottom of the boat.

The body did not move and Henneberry did not see his face, but he suspected immediately it might be the fugitive Dzhokhar Tsarnaev. He returned to his house, where he called 9-1-1.

Within minutes, three armed police officers converged on the backyard boat. They were joined by others as the flashing lights of police cars filled Franklin Street. Police escorted Henneberry and his wife to a neighbor's house to get them out of harm's way.

Dzhokhar had been lying in the boat for about 15 hours. It would take negotiators from the FBI's Hostage Rescue Team nearly three hours to convince Dzhokhar to surrender.

The police arsenal included large black armored vehicles, K-9 unit dogs and a robotic tank they used to peel back the tarpaulin on the Slip Away. A forward-looking infrared thermal imaging camera on a State Police helicopter was used to penetrate the boat's cover and hull to show Dzhokhar's heat image inside.

Police approached slowly, methodically to surround the boat. Some of the bomb-sniffing dogs were used to search the area for explosives.

Chatter on a police scanner said, "we have movement in the boat." The chatter reported incorrectly that there was a "fire on the boat."

One of the speakers on the scanner said, "He is laying prone position head towards the sun in the middle of the boat ... he's moving."

Dzhokhar pushed the tarp up, prompting some police to believe he would fire a gun at them. Police responded with a volley of about 30 shots that one resident said sounded like "firecrackers."

The gunfire stopped only when the police superintendent on the scene shouted for them to cease fire.

Later evidence showed Dzhokhar was unarmed, which also disproved initial police reports he might have shot himself in a suicide attempt.

Residents who witnessed the shooting said police threw flash grenades to stun Dzhokhar. They overheard an FBI negotiator with a bullhorn say, "We know you're in there. Come out on your own terms. Come out with your hands up."

The Boston Globe contacted residents of the neighborhood during the standoff. The newspaper quoted one of them saying, "We're seeing every officer rushing to the corner. We've heard gunshots. We've got cops in bulletproof vests and an ambulance is there with someone carrying out a stretcher."

Dzhokhar crawled out of the boat just before 9 p.m. Blood on his face, his neck and thigh showed he was seriously injured. Police described the neck wound as a slicing injury that might have been inflicted by shrapnel from an explosion.

One witness reported, "His left arm and left leg hung over the boat's side. He appeared to struggle for consciousness." He was "hauled down to the grassy ground" by a SWAT officer.

Other police rushed up to surround him, search him, strip off his clothes and to handcuff him. A photograph from the scene showed medical staff examining his wounds.

Shortly afterward, chatter on the police scanner said, "Suspect in custody." A crowd of onlookers beyond the police line cheered as officers escorted the handcuffed Dzhokhar away.

Just over an hour later, President Obama released a statement congratulating police officers who arrested Dzhokhar and added, "We've closed an important chapter in this tragedy."

Only after the arrest of the bloodied Dzhokhar would Payack learn that his appeal to surrender might have played an important role. An FBI agent who negotiated through loudspeaker messages to Dzhokhar as he lay wounded in the backyard boat sent a text message to Payack.

The message said, "Thanks coach." It ended by saying, "I actually told him that you'd like to see him to come out peacefully. I think it helped."

Payack still showed conflicted feelings about the prime

suspect months after he was arrested. The coach remembered the respect he had for Dzhokhar but could not come to grips with the crime he was accused of committing.

"You want to think evil has an evil face, but he didn't have an evil face," Payack said for this report.

"People say we harbored terrorists, but we didn't harbor terrorists," Payack said. "I think he's honestly a good person but then things changed."

On the other hand, Payack acknowledges Dzhokhar stands accused of doing what he called "the most evil thing" for which he must accept responsibility.

"He's a man," Payack said. "You can't just say his brother did it. There are some people who are thinking, it wasn't his fault. But if you have a gun in your hand or a bomb in your hand, then it's your fault."

"How can somebody change the way he did," Payack asked.

As President Obama's statement hit the airwaves, police discovered another surprise from Dzhokhar — one that might have sealed his fate for a later trial.

Inside a panel of the boat riddled with bullet holes where he was hiding, Dzhokhar left a poorly punctuated, handwritten message with a marker pen.

"The U.S. government is killing our innocent civilians," he wrote. "I don't like killing innocent people." But the message added, "I can't stand to see such evil go unpunished."

The message continued, saying, "We Muslims are one body. You hurt one, you hurt us all. When you attack one Muslim, you attack all Muslims."

He described the Boston Marathon bombing victims as "collateral damage," similar to Muslims killed by Americans in Iraq and Afghanistan. He implied Americans were "infidels."

He wrote about his brother, who he already knew was dead. He described him as a martyr. He said he did not grieve for him because he knew he would see him again in paradise soon after his own death.

"The ummah [Muslim people] is beginning to rise," Dzhokhar wrote. "Know you are fighting men who look into the barrel of your gun and see heaven, now how can you compete with that."

He also wrote slogans inside the boat, such as "Praise Allah" and "Fuck America."

THE LAWYERS AND JUDGES TAKE OVER

DZHOKHAR WAS TAKEN to Beth Israel Deaconess Medical Center, where his brother had died less than a day earlier. After initial treatment in the emergency department, he was put into an intensive care unit. Doctors announced his condition as serious but stable. His condition was upgraded to fair three days later.

Nurses said he cried for two days after waking up. One police bullet pierced his mouth. A bullet wound also damaged the pharynx of his throat, leaving him barely able to speak. He communicated by nodding his head or writing notes.

His injuries included a skull-base fracture, damage to part of his C1 vertebrae, a middle ear injury, soft tissue lesions and a small vascular injury.

Initially, he was questioned without being read his Miranda rights. Normally, a reading of Miranda rights is a required procedure when police arrest anyone. Dzhokhar's case was different because the Justice Department claimed a public safety exception to Miranda rights when a prisoner might represent an ongoing threat.

During the initial questioning, Dzhokhar admitted his involvement in the marathon bombings. He said he and his brother were religiously motivated and were retaliating for U.S. attacks on Muslims in Iraq and Afghanistan. He acknowledged that he and Tamerlan wanted to set a bomb in New York City's Times Square. They started planning the Times Square bombing during the carjacking that the escaped vehicle owner reported to police.

Dzhokhar said he was inspired by videos from al Qaeda propagandist Anwar al-Awlaki, who emboldened the suspects in the failed 2010 Times Square car bombing attempt.

Neither the initial interrogation nor subsequent investigation showed Dzhokhar was as radical as his brother. The investigation was based on a review of his computer files, statements to friends, his Internet searches that revealed few visits to websites advocating holy war and his lack of association with organized political or religious groups.

Instead, police concluded Dzhokhar was more like a naïve common criminal who was led by the domineering influence of his older brother.

Dzhokhar was formally charged at his bedside on April 22 with "using and conspiring to use a weapon of mass destruction resulting in death" and with "malicious destruction of property resulting in death."

At that point, the Justice Department relented and had a federal magistrate read him his Miranda rights. He nodded to answer most of the judge's questions. The only word Dzhokhar was able to utter was "no" when police asked him whether he could afford a lawyer.

When he recovered enough to be moved, Dzhokhar was taken by U.S. marshals on April 26 to a federal prison near Boston called the Federal Medical Center, Devens.

Even his questioning by interrogators was different than most prisoners. The same kind of High-Value Interrogation Group that questions radical Islamic detainees at the Guantanamo prison in Cuba was brought in. Their interrogators are drawn from the CIA, the Defense Department and the FBI.

Dzhokhar refused to comment after being read his Miranda rights. Like many prisoners facing prosecution, he declined any further cooperation with the investigation or statements that could be used as evidence against him at trial.

His court-appointed defense team included federal public defender Miriam Conrad, anti-death penalty attorney Judy Clarke and William Fick.

The prosecutors were Justice Department heavyweights. They included William Weinreb and Aloke Chakravarty from the Anti-Terrorism and National Security Unit of the Boston U.S. Attorney's Office.

On June 27, Dzhokhar A. Tsarnaev was indicted by a federal grand jury in Boston on charges that could bring him life in prison or the death penalty.

Among the most serious charges in the 30-count indictment were use of a weapon of mass destruction resulting in death and the murders of four people.

Allegations in the indictment cleared up some of the unanswered questions about the bombing. They also laid out the government's case against Tsarnaev.

The indictment said Tsarnaev wrote a confession on the inside of the boat where he was hiding in a suburban Boston back yard when police shot him. The message said, "I don't like killing innocent people" but that the U.S. government's attacks against Muslims justified his actions.

"The U.S. government is killing our innocent civilians," Tsarnaev wrote. "I can't stand to see such evil go unpunished ... We Muslims are one body, you hurt one, you hurt us all.

"Stop killing our innocent people, we will stop," he allegedly wrote.

U.S. Attorney Carmen J. Ortiz said at a press conference that she had recently met with survivors and families of victims of the bombings.

"Their strength is extraordinary and we will do everything that we can to pursue justice not only on their behalf but on the behalf of all us," Ortiz said.

In addition to the bombings, the indictment accused Tsarnaev and his brother, Tamerlan, of killing Massachusetts Institute of Technology police officer Sean Collier.

The government investigation revealed how the brothers used the Internet to learn to prepare the bombs, as well as to become inspired by Islamist rhetoric.

Dzhokhar Tsarnaev downloaded propaganda from extremist Islamic web sites that advised Muslims to resist governments that invade Arab countries. Some of the propaganda came from Anwar al-Awlaki, an American citizen who turned against his home country to become a senior member of al Qaeda in Yemen. He was killed in a U.S. drone strike in 2011.

Technical details about how to build the bombs came from Volume 1 of the radical Islamist online magazine "Inspire," according to the indictment.

DZHOKHAR MAKES A COURT APPEARANCE

ON JULY 10, 2013, DZHOKHAR was brought to federal court for the first time in Boston for arraignment on 30 charges before U.S. Magistrate Judge Marianne Bowler. He pleaded not guilty to all the charges.

He faced other charges from Middlesex County for his alleged complicity in the murder of MIT Police Officer Collier.

On Oct. 7, 2013, a Middlesex Superior Court judge in Woburn issued a default warrant for the arrest of Dzhokhar. A default warrant means the case against him for murder will remain open until the federal case against him is resolved. The U.S. Justice Department refused to let him be tried in the state court until they finished their own case.

In addition to the murder charge in the death of Collier, state prosecutors charged Dzhokhar with intent to murder for participating in the shootout that killed his brother.

The procedures in federal and state court were surrounded by controversy. Some Republican members of Congress had demanded that Dzhokhar be held as an enemy combatant who could be questioned by military interrogators without a right of representation by counsel.

Republican senators Lindsey Graham, John McCain and Kelly Ayotte put out a statement saying, "We continue to face threats from radical Islamists in small cells and large groups throughout the world. They have as their primary focus killing as many Americans as possible, preferably within the United States. We must never lose sight of this fact and act appropriately within our laws and values."

Dzhokhar was saved from the rough treatment of being classified as an enemy combatant by the fact he gained American citizenship on Sept. 11, 2012.

The Republican senators argued that citizenship alone should not protect him. They tried to draw support for their position from the 2004 Supreme Court ruling in Hamdi v. Rumsfeld. Yaser Esam Hamdi was a dual U.S. and Egyptian citizen captured by American forces in 2001 in Afghanistan, where he was accused of being an enemy combatant.

The Supreme Court ruled that as an American citizen, Hamdi was entitled to rights of due process and to challenge accusations of being an enemy combatant in court. But the court added, "There is no bar to this nation's holding one of its own citizens as enemy combatant."

The Obama administration put an end to any chance for Dzhokhar's enemy combatant status when White House spokesman Jay Carney said during a press conference, "We will prosecute this terrorist through our civilian system of justice."

Other terrorism suspects had been prosecuted since the September 11 attacks in civilian courts, Carney said.

"The system has repeatedly proven that it can successfully handle the threat we continue to face," Carney said.

Dzhokhar's first appearance in federal court on July 10, 2013 was punctuated with all the security and television cameras of a presidential visit. Scuba divers checked the nearby river for bombs; A Boston Police Harbor Unit boat patrolled the waters and 20 MIT police officers stood at attention. Dzhokhar arrived at the courthouse hours before the arraignment in a four-vehicle motorcade.

On television, heartrending stories from victims accompanied reports of Dzhokhar showing up in court wearing a cast on his left arm, shackles and an orange prison jumpsuit.

"I wanted more than anything just to stand up on two feet," J.P. Norden, who lost a leg in the bombing, told ABC News.

Witnesses in the courtroom described Dzhokhar as fidgety as he pleaded not guilty to all of the 30 charges against him. He spoke with a Russian accent. He turned toward the crowd in the packed courtroom several times during the hearing.

U.S. District Court Judge Bowler mentioned that 30 victims and their family members were present in the courtroom during the arraignment. Along with them were Dzhokhar's two sisters wearing Muslim clothing.

The judge refused to accept defense attorney Judy Clarke's attempt to plead not guilty on behalf of Dzhokhar to all the charges. Instead, she asked that Dzhokhar speak for himself as each of the charges was read. He said "not guilty" seven times in a clear voice, which surprised some journalists who believed the gunshot wound to his neck might have impaired his ability to speak.

His eyes appeared to be irritated and dark around the edges. His face was slightly swollen. He moved his jaw awkwardly in what appeared to be nervous gestures.

At one point, he appeared to smirk, which some witnesses interpreted as disrespect but others said showed nervousness.

Several times, he turned toward his sisters and smiled as they cried throughout the hearing. As U.S. marshals led him out of the courtroom after the seven-minute arraignment, Dzhokhar blew a kiss toward his sisters.

MIT Police Chief John DiFava told ABC News that he saw "absolutely no remorse" in Dzhokhar.

ABC News also interviewed the young suspect's mother at her home in Russia. Zubeidat Tsarnaeva, who had an open arrest warrant pending against her in Massachusetts on suspicion of shoplifting, continued to claim that her son was innocent.

She said she would like to travel to the United States but only if she knew she would be allowed to see her son. "His fate is in Allah's hands," she told ABC News.

Dzhokhar returned to a 10-foot by 10-foot cell where he was being kept in near-solitary confinement in a segregated unit. He was on 23-hour-a-day lockdown, with only one hour a day for recreation outside the cell.

He was denied access to television, radio, prayer with other inmates, family photos and visits by anyone other than his immediate family and attorneys.

Days after the July 2013 hearing, Rolling Stone magazine published a cover story that featured Dzhokhar. It was entitled: "The Bomber: How a Popular, Promising Student Was Failed by His Family, Fell into Radical Islam and Became a Monster."

The story traced Dzhokhar's life, education and family as told by his friends and co-workers. It portrayed him as a largely likeable and sympathetic person, almost right up to the moment the bombs exploded at the Boston Marathon. The August 2013 issue of Rolling Stone came with a photo of Dzhokhar on the cover that made him look like the rock stars commonly found in other editions of the magazine.

The story drew immediate criticism in the Boston community.

Massachusetts State Police sergeant Sean Murphy said "glamorizing the face of terror is not just insulting to the family members of those killed in the line of duty, it also could be an incentive to those who may be unstable to do something to get their face on the cover of Rolling Stone magazine."

Boston Mayer Thomas Menino wrote a letter to Rolling Stone publisher Jann Wenner that said, "Your August 3 cover rewards a terrorist with celebrity treatment. It is ill-conceived, at best, and re-affirms a terrible message that destruction gains fame for killers and their 'causes.' There may be valuable journalism behind your sensational treatment, though we can't know because almost all you released is the cover.

"To respond to you in anger is to feed into your obvious marketing strategy. So, I write to you instead to put the focus where you could have: on the brave and strong survivors and on the thousands of people — their family and friends, volunteers, first responders, doctors, nurses and donors — who have come to their side. Among those we lost, those who survived, and those who help carry them forward, there are artists and musicians and dancers and writers. They have dreams and plans. They struggle and strive. The survivors of the Boston attacks deserve Rolling Stone cover stories, though I no longer feel that Rolling Stone deserves them."

Rolling Stone columnist Matt Taibbi responded to critics by saying they misunderstood the magazine's role as a news organization, apparently because they incorrectly associated it only with the glamour of the music industry.

The magazine's editors posted a statement saying, "Our hearts go out to the victims of the Boston Marathon bombing, and our thoughts are always with them and their families. The cover story we are publishing this week falls within the traditions of journalism and Rolling Stone's long-standing commitment to serious and thoughtful coverage of the most important political and cultural issues of our day. The fact that Dzhokhar Tsarnaev is young, and in the same age group as many of our readers, makes it all the more important for us to examine the complexities of this issue and gain a more complete understanding of how a tragedy like this happens."

The editors' explanation was too little and too late to appease members of the Boston community. Many retailers, such as CVS Pharmacy and BJ's Wholesale Club, announced they would not sell the August 2013 issue of Rolling Stone.

Nevertheless, newsstand sales of the issue doubled to about 120,000. The following December, Ad Week magazine named the cover as the "Hottest Cover of the Year."

Meanwhile, Dzhokhar's attorneys were filing motions with the federal court to have his jail restrictions eased. They said the tight detention restrictions, called "special administrative measures," were "unlawful and unwarranted" considering that Dzhokhar created no threat while incarcerated.

Dzhokhar has not "done or said anything since his arrest to commit violence, incite violence or engage in communications that pose a security threat," the defense team said in its motion.

Nevertheless, "He is confined to his cell except for legal visits and very limited access to a small outdoor enclosure, on weekdays, weather permitting," the motion for eased restrictions said. "The purported basis for these conditions lies in the crimes he is alleged to have committed prior to arrest, not any behavior during his confinement."

Although their client had not been convicted of a crime, his closely controlled detention was "effectively punitive," the attorneys wrote.

"The negative effects of isolation on detainees are well-documented," the motion said. "Indeed, the United Nations identifies long-term solitary confinement as a form of torture."

In addition, the special administrative procedures interfered with their ability to properly represent their client because of his inability to communicate with people helping his case, Dzhokhar's attorneys said.

His mail showed no "jihadist" tendencies or contacts, the defense lawyers said. Much of it consisted of letters from well-wishers who urged him to "repent and convert to Christianity."

The American Civil Liberties Union filed a "friend-of-the-court" brief that agreed with everything the defense attorneys said. The brief accused prosecutors and jailers of depriving Dzhokhar of his Sixth Amendment right to representation by counsel by such tight restrictions that interfered with the attorneys' ability to gather evidence.

Special administrative measures generally are used with the most dangerous criminal defendants. They have included Richard Reid, who is accused of trying to blow up a commercial airliner flying from Paris to Miami on Dec. 22, 2001, by igniting a bomb in his shoe. He is serving a life sentence in a U.S. super maximum security prison.

"American Taliban" fighter John Walker Lindh also was placed under special administrative measures. He was captured by American forces in Afghanistan in November 2001 while fighting for the extremist Islamic group known as the Taliban. He is serving a 20-year prison sentence.

The heavy jail restrictions were placed on Dzhokhar in response to an Aug. 27 memo from U.S. Attorney General Eric H. Holder Jr. to the director of the U.S. Bureau of Prisons. The memo was headlined with the words "Limited Official Use."

It portrayed Dzhokhar as creating an ongoing threat of terrorism if he were allowed outside contact while imprisoned.

Dzhokhar told FBI agents after he was arrested that he still was "committed to jihad and expressed hope that his actions would inspire others to engage in violent jihad," the memo said. Even after the marathon bombings, Dzhokhar and Tamerlan Tsarnaev "made additional bombs" and convinced their friends to "attempt to destroy evidence related to the attack."

Dzhokhar "employed operational tradecraft" for terrorists and "purchased a dedicated cellphone" to speak secretly with his brother after the bombings, the Justice Department memo said. He tried to destroy the cellphone and to throw away a bomb detonator to hide the evidence.

His uncontrolled communications could "result in death or serious bodily injury" to other persons, the memo said. Regarding his statements to the FBI of dedication to jihad, the memo said, "There is no indication that Tsarnaev's intentions have changed since."

Part of the evidence against Dzhokhar was based on the message he scrawled inside the backyard boat before police shot at him.

Prosecutors said it showed a lack of remorse and an ongoing threat. His defense attorneys said Dzhokhar intended it only as a farewell statement as he prepared to die.

"There is no express call for others to take up arms," the defense attorneys said in a court filing. "On their face, Mr. Tsarnaev's alleged words simply state the motive for his actions, a declaration in anticipation of his own death."

A federal judge who reviewed the Justice Department memo and defense team's response largely denied the request for easier jail restrictions. The judge continued to say Dzhokhar should be held without bail.

He also ruled the American Civil Liberties Union should have no further right to participate in the case. The advocacy group was filing a "volunteered submission by non-parties" the court should not consider, the judge wrote.

Meanwhile, suburban police near Dzhokhar's neighborhood were left to deal with what Lieutenant Michael Lawn of the Watertown Police Department called "a whole different normal here."

The Watertown Police Department is "four square miles and 65 officers," he said almost sevens months after the bombings. "I don't think there's a day that has gone by since this event that we haven't dealt with it in some way."

A MURDER INVESTIGATION REOPENS

AS THE BOMBING investigation delved deeper into the lives of Tamerlan and Dzhokhar Tsarnaev, new evidence prompted police to review a triple murder the previous September.

Three men were brutally murdered in Waltham, Mass., on Sept. 11, 2011 — the 10th anniversary of the 9/11 terrorist attacks against the United States.

Two of the men, Raphael Teken and Erik Weissman, were Jewish. The third, Brendan Mess, was their roommate.

Their throats were cut from ear to ear and their heads pulled back. Police said they nearly were decapitated.

The investigation was complicated by the fact a simple motive like robbery did not appear to be the reason. About seven pounds of marijuana were spread over the bodies. About $5,000 in cash was left behind strewn on the floor and on top of the dead men.

For nearly two years, police had no clues to the assailant. They described the murders as a random crime. After the April 15, 2013 bombings, they revisited their evidence to discover what they call "forensic hits" to Tamerlan Tsarnaev. A trace of his cellphone records showed he had made a call near the murder scene on the night of the killings.

The break in the murders coincided with the police and FBI investigation into Tamerlan's network of friends, acquaintances and coworkers following the marathon bombings. They found that Brendan Mess had once been Tamerlan's roommate and trained with him for boxing. Mess was helping Tamerlan transition more into mixed martial arts as his boxing career fizzled.

Mess and his roommates had ordered a home delivery of dinner from nearby Gerry's Italian Kitchen at 8:54 p.m. on the night they were murdered. A delivery woman arrived shortly afterward but received no answer to her knock at the door. Mess also failed to answer the cellphone from which he placed the order.

Mess' girlfriend found the bodies the next day. A police investigator told ABC News the murder scene was "the worst bloodbath I have ever seen in a long law enforcement career."

There was no forced entry and neighbors said they heard no noise indicating violence, even though the windows were open.

In other words, the murderer most likely was someone known to the victims who they let into the house. The girlfriend, whose name was not released by police, told investigators Tamerlan had sometimes visited the apartment.

Tamerlan did not attend Mess' funeral, which seemed unusual after their apparent friendship. He also stopped attending the martial arts gym where the men had trained together.

Further investigation eventually led the FBI to Ibragim Todashev, a former martial arts training buddy of Tamerlan. Cellphone records connected the two men, which helped the FBI trace 27-year-old Todashev to his new home near the Universal Studios theme park in Orlando, Florida.

Todashev lived long enough to confess during an interview at his home that Tamerlan killed the three men in Waltham during a drug theft, the FBI reported. They were concerned the men would identify them to police. To keep their silence, Tamerlan and Todashev killed them, according to the FBI.

Other reports indicated Todashev was present during the murders but Tamerlan acted alone in killing the men.

Todashev, a Chechen who was granted asylum in the United States in 2008, met Tamerlan while he lived in Boston and hung out with other Chechen expatriates. The cellphone calls traced by the FBI consisted of simple pleasantries, such as hello, how are you and how's your family.

Even more revealing was the fact police were able to match DNA evidence they found at the murder scene to Todashev. The FBI said it notified him they would like to interview him only two days before he planned to fly home to Russia.

The FBI reported that when an FBI agent asked Todashev to sign a confession just after midnight, he became belligerent. He grabbed a knife in his kitchen to attack the agent, who shot and killed him.

The agent sustained non-life threatening injuries in a struggle with Todashev, the FBI reported.

The FBI released a statement afterward saying, "The agent, two Massachusetts State Police troopers and other law enforcement personnel were interviewing an individual in connection with the Boston Marathon bombing investigation when a violent confrontation was initiated by the individual. During the confrontation, the individual was killed."

The reopened Waltham murder investigation also raised suspicions about where Tamerlan got the Ruger 9 mm semi-automatic handgun he used the night he was killed.

Mess' girlfriend, an African immigrant, told investigators Mess kept a similar gun in his apartment. Police told her after the Waltham murder investigation they could not find the gun.

Police initially suspected the missing gun was the same one used to kill MIT Officer Sean Collier and the same one Tamerlan shot at other police hours later.

Later, they realized the gun appeared to come from a friend of Dzhokhar named Stephen Silva. Prosecutors never claimed Silva was directly involved in the marathon bombings. Their indictment said that as soon as a few weeks before the bombings, in February 2013, Silva possessed the gun.

The indictment did not explain exactly how or why he allegedly gave the gun to the Tsarnaevs. It only accused him of illegally possessing it and unrelated drug charges.

Silva, 21, who wanted to go to law school and become a public defender, pleaded not guilty to the charges on Aug. 6 in federal court in Boston but later agreed to cooperate with prosecutors in exchange for a guilty plea and a lighter sentence.

Mess' girlfriend revealed a small irony after one of Tamerlan's social visits to the Waltham apartment a few weeks before the murders. Tamerlan told Mess the FBI had placed him on their watch list as a possible terrorist. Mess and his girlfriend laughed at such a preposterous idea.

Todashev's father gave a different account of his son's death that hinted at an FBI cover-up.

Abdulbaki Todashev wrote a letter to President Obama in December 2013 asking for a complete account of his son's death. He admitted his son knew Tamerlan but denied he was involved in any kind of crime.

He also contradicted the FBI's report that implied Ibragim Todashev was trying to flee to Russia. He said his son voluntarily went to the FBI office in Orlando four times to speak with agents before they came to his apartment May 21 until just after midnight on May 22 and shot him.

An investigation by Boston's WBUR public radio station revealed some details that could embarrass the FBI. It said Todashev was interviewed at his condominium for nearly five hours by an FBI agent and two Massachusetts State Police officers.

After several hours, Todashev reportedly told them, "I was there but I didn't do the murders," according to unidentified sources quoted by WBUR. The FBI agent and police officers also noted Todashev was agitated after the nearly five-hour interrogation.

When it came time for him to sign a confession, he reportedly shoved a table into the FBI agent, knocking him down and giving him a cut on the head that required stitches. One of the troopers said Todashev approached him with a pipe as if he were about to strike him.

The FBI agent reportedly fired three shots that hit Todashev, knocking him down. But Todashev got up, prompting the FBI agent to fire four more shots that ended his life at 12:15 a.m. on May 22.

Todashev's family displayed photos of his dead body to the news media that showed one of the shots hit him near the top of his head. His father said the shot indicated his son might have been executed. He also claimed his son was shot 13 times and suffered "hematomas," or bruises, possibly indicating he was beaten.

Abdulbaki Todashev's letter to Obama said, "Did my son know that he had the right to remain silent or did he have rights at all, including the right to live? Being a citizen of another country he might not be aware of the laws as he was only 27 years old and wanted to live so much. No, they left no chances for him inflicting 13 gunshot wounds and multiple hematomas on his body.

"After what FBI agents have done to him whatever excuses they come up with nobody would believe them because my son is dead and cannot talk for himself. They did it deliberately so that he can never speak and never take part in court hearings. They put pressure on my son's friends to prevent them from coming to the court and speaking the truth.

"I rely on you, Mr. President, and hope that the prosecutor's office and the court do not let the agencies conducting internal investigation on this case prevent the truth from coming to light so that at least some part of our grief, caused by the murder of our son, is relieved, and that the murderers stand trial instead of sit in their desk chairs."

THE DEATH PENALTY

ANY QUESTIONS ABOUT the degree of the Boston community's outrage over the marathon bombings were answered when the Massachusetts U.S. Attorney's office acknowledged it was seriously considering the death penalty against Dzhokhar Tsarnaev.

The decision was based significantly on interviews with bombing victims, who were asked their preference for a punishment.

In most other states, no one would be surprised by a decision to seek the death penalty. Massachusetts was theoretically different.

There is no death penalty in Massachusetts. In fact, surveys of Massachusetts residents show many of them prefer life imprisonment as the worst punishment that could be imposed on criminal convicts. Seventeen other states and the District of Columbia also do not allow the death penalty.

However, Dzhokhar was to be prosecuted in federal court, which does not need to follow state laws or procedures.

Since the first execution of a convicted murderer in 1630 until the last one in 1947, Massachusetts executed 345 people, including 26 for witchcraft. Until 1951, state law required a mandatory death penalty for first degree, or premeditated, murder. State lawmakers changed the law to allow the jury to decide. Juries sentenced several convicted murderers to death after 1951 but none were executed.

Massachusetts has flip-flopped in court cases and proposed legislation that sought to reinstate the death penalty. Each time, the proposals went down to defeat either by ruling of the state's Supreme Judicial Court or by a vote of the legislature. The last time the issue arose in the Massachusetts General Court, or state legislature, was in November 2007, when the House of Representatives overwhelmingly voted against a bill to reinstate the death penalty by a 46-110 margin.

The U.S. Supreme Court struck down the death penalty for most states only for a few years with the 1972 case of Furman v. Georgia. The court's ruling said Georgia's death penalty was "arbitrary and capricious" in the way it was done. The court accused the state of "cruel and unusual punishment."

In 1976, the Supreme Court reinstated state death penalties when it ruled in the case of Gregg v. Georgia that Georgia's revised capital murder law included enough safeguards to avoid the previous violations of due process. Other states responded with revisions to their procedures that allowed them to execute murderers.

Regardless of what Georgia, Massachusetts or any other state says, federal courts can decide for themselves when capital murder leads to the death penalty.

The federal government has allowed the death penalty since 1988. The most high profile of the three people executed under the federal death penalty since 1988 was Timothy McVeigh, who was convicted of bombing the federal office building in Oklahoma City in 1995.

Now the federal authority came to rest on the prosecution of Dzhokhar Tsarnaev.

His defense attorneys tried desperately to block a possible death penalty. They notified U.S. District Court Judge George A. O'Toole Jr. that they intended to oppose any Justice Department decision to seek the death penalty while asking for more time to prepare their court filings.

However, the judge said there was little he could do to help them.

"The decision ... rests with the prosecution," O'Toole wrote in a four-page Oct. 18 ruling. The defense can ask prosecutors for more time but "it is not required by any constitutional, statutory or decisional rule of law. It is essentially a matter of grace."

Even more daunting in the deadline dispute were the words of Assistant U.S. Attorney William D. Weinreb, who filed a motion against the Tsarnaev defense team's request for more time. His explanation to the judge left little doubt prosecutors were likely to recommend a death penalty.

"[Tsarnaev] is accused of one of the most serious terrorist attacks against civilians on American soil since September 11, 2001," Weinreb wrote. "He is charged with brutally murdering two women and a small child; maiming, blinding and deafening scores of others; carjacking a victim then robbing him; executing a police officer; and then attempting to murder other police officers with bombs and gunfire. The victims, who were most affected by the charged crimes, as well as the general public, are entitled to see justice done in this case without undue delay."

The defense team did win a small victory with its pre-trial motions. The federal judge agreed to give them more time to decide whether they wanted a change of venue.

A change of venue refers to switching the trial to a different court far from the site of the crime. Venue changes are typically granted when emotions in a community are running so high that it would be nearly impossible to find an impartial jury.

Originally, the deadline for defense lawyers to file a change of venue motion was Feb. 28, 2014. Judge O'Toole said he would extend the deadline after the lawyers said they needed time to research a more appropriate venue.

The exchange of pre-trial motions also gave a glimpse of the defense strategy Dzhokhar's attorneys were likely to argue.

The defense attorneys filed a motion asking the judge to order prosecutors to turn over their evidence of Tamerlan's involvement in the Sept. 11, 2011 triple murder in Waltham. They argued in their motion that Tamerlan's involvement in the murders was "mitigating information" that is critical to Dzhokhar's defense.

Although they did not say it directly, the defense attorneys appeared to be preparing to argue Dzhokhar lacked the "willfulness" required for criminal conviction or at least the death penalty.

Willfulness, according to Black's Law Dictionary, refers to an "unlawful intent" and "intending the result which actually comes to pass."

However, if Dzhokhar was Tamerlan's "puppy dog" as his boxing coach described him, then perhaps Dzhokhar was merely following the intentions of his domineering and murderous older brother. Perhaps Tamerlan should be blamed rather than his impressionable younger brother who still was a teenager when bombs killed and maimed at the Boston Marathon.

Without evidence of willfulness, any prosecution argument for the death penalty would fall apart. Instead, any criminal penalty could be no more than the routine punishment of a naïve kid in the wrong place at the wrong time.

Some legal experts wondered whether Dzhokhar's defense team would focus almost entirely on trying to save his life instead of arguing his innocence.

Regarding a good defense strategy, "There isn't one," said David Rossman, director of Boston University Law School's criminal law clinical programs. Instead, Dzhokhar should plead guilty and use his evidence to get the easiest sentence possible.

"That's his best bet," Rossman said. "He's got some of the best lawyers in the country. One of the things lawyers do is educate their clients. And he's a kid. He's malleable in that way. If his brother could influence him in one direction, then I think his lawyers could influence him in another direction."

Rossman speculated that although his defense attorneys might present evidence of Tamerlan's overbearing influence on his brother, they would be unlikely to win acquittal.

"It would be very, very, very difficult to massage the influence the older brother had over the younger brother into a defense on the merits," said Rossman, who has represented criminal defendants before the U.S. Supreme Court.

On the other hand, the defense attorneys might be facing a stubborn client who will allow them only to argue he is innocent. In that case, trying to prove a lack of willfulness because of Tamerlan's influence might be his only — albeit weak — defense, Rossman said.

"It may be that this kid wants a defense on the merits even though it has no chance, in which case the lawyers might be forced to do that," Rossman said.

If Dzhokhar will settle only for a not guilty plea, "they'll have to take the least bad of all the terrible defenses that are out there for him," Rossman said.

Regardless of the defense strategy, Rossman said the surrounding facts create a high probability Dzhokhar will have to argue against a death penalty.

"I think it's very high and the reason is because this is such a notorious event that captured the nation's attention in a way that hasn't happened since 9/11," Rossman said.

There are two parts to death penalty trials. First, a jury decides whether the defendant is guilty or innocent. If Dzhokhar is convicted, the trial moves to a sentencing phase. A death penalty sentence requires a unanimous jury decision.

Massachusetts jurors have departed from their state's no

death penalty policy previously in federal criminal cases to sentence defendants to death.

"I think it can happen again," Rossman said.

Seventy percent of Americans favored the death penalty for Dzhokhar in a May 2013 Washington Post-ABC News poll. However, only 33 percent of Massachusetts residents surveyed by the Boston Globe in September 2013 wanted the death penalty for him. Another 57 percent of Massachusetts respondents said Dzhokhar should get life in prison without parole.

On Jan. 30, 2014, the mystery and speculation over the punishment the Justice Department would seek ended.

Attorney General Eric Holder issued a statement saying, "After consideration of the relevant facts, the applicable regulations and the submissions made by the defendant's counsel, I have determined that the United States will seek the death penalty in this matter. The nature of the conduct at issue and the resultant harm compel this decision."

Holder's announcement was followed by a statement from Massachusetts Governor Deval Patrick, who said, "One way or another, based on the evidence, Tsarnaev will die in prison.

"In each milestone of this case — today's announcement, the trial and every other significant step in the justice process — the people hurt by the Marathon bombings and the rest of us so shocked by it will relive the tragedy."

Also on Jan. 30, 2014, prosecutors filed court documents that summarized their trial strategy for the death penalty.

They said they would show the victims died while Dzhokhar committed another crime by setting off a bomb, which is a prerequisite for proving felony murder. They also said they would prove Dzhokhar planned the crime, which is evidence of the kind of premeditated murder that can invoke the death penalty.

"Dzhokhar Tsarnaev targeted the Boston Marathon, an iconic event that draws large crowds of men, women and children to its final stretch, making it especially susceptible to the act and effects of terrorism," the prosecution's eight-page document filed in federal court in Boston said.

Dzhokhar "enjoyed the freedoms of a United States citizen [then] betrayed his allegiance to the United States by killing and maiming people in the United States," the prosecutors said. They added that he "demonstrated a lack of remorse."

Beyond the name-calling, prosecutors gave clues about how they would lock horns with defense attorneys at trial.

They said they would prove the killings by Tsarnaev were intentional, that he willingly participated in the bombings and that he knew his actions could kill other persons.

In other words, a pivotal issue would be whether the bombings really were Dzhokhar's will or whether he merely tagged along to follow the will of his bulldog older brother.

In any case, Tamerlan Tsarnaev would haunt the proceedings.

Further proof the defense would try to show Tamerlan was the real culprit came from their pre-trial motions. The lawyers wanted the court to order the FBI to turn over records of its requests to Tamerlan to be an informant against Muslims.

"We seek this information based on our belief that these contacts were among the precipitating events for Tamerlan's actions during the week of April 15, 2013," their court filing said.

"We base this information from our client's family and other sources that the FBI made more than one visit to talk with Anzor [his father], Zubeidat [his mother] and Tamerlan, questioned Tamerlan about his Internet searches and asked him to be an informant, reporting on the Chechen and Muslim community".

The defense lawyers said Tamerlan might have interpreted any FBI requests to be an informant as pressure that "increased his paranoia and distress."

They also hinted at their defense strategy of portraying Dzhokhar as a victim rather than a villain.

"Any surveillance, evidence or interviews showing that Tamerlan's pursuit of jihad predated Dzhokhar's would tend to support the theory that Tamerlan was the main instigator of the tragic events that followed," the defense team's court filing said.

They also said information not yet revealed about Dzhokhar's "formative environment and relative moral culpability" and possible "psychological domination" by his older brother would help their case against the death penalty.

The FBI declined to comment on the defense lawyers' filing but did release a copy of its Oct. 18, 2013 statement that said, "The Tsarnaev brothers were never sources for the FBI, nor did the FBI attempt to recruit them as sources."

On Feb. 12, 2014, the federal judge presiding in the case set the trial date for Nov. 3, 2014.

Dzhokhar's attorneys tried to argue for more time, saying they must collect evidence spread over two continents while battling prosecutors they said were reluctant to turn over important information.

Defense attorney Judy Clarke said "meeting the trial date will be impossible."

Judge O'Toole ignored her plea, saying, "I think this is a realistic and fair date."

TAMERLAN'S WIDOW

LIKE SO MANY crimes that create public outrage, the Boston Marathon bombings cast suspicion on anyone associated with the Tsarnaevs. The question left for the courts and public opinion to decide was whether they really were accomplices or merely incidental figures drawn into the tragedy through naïveté.

One of them was Katherine Russell, the widow of Tamerlan, who came from an upright American home that was most notable for its lack of controversy.

Her father was an emergency room doctor and her mother a nurse. She was born in Texas on Feb. 6, 1989, into a Christian home. The family later moved to Rhode Island.

She graduated at the top of her class in 2007 from North Kingstown High School, where she was known for being a talented painter, illustrator and saxophone player. She tried to put together a portfolio of her drawings to help her find employment as an illustrator, but the job never materialized. She often dressed like any other teenaged girl, wearing jeans and pullover shirts with her brown hair hanging over the collar. Her friends called her Katie. She wrote in her yearbook that she was considering joining the Peace Corps.

First, she had a minor brush with the law. She was arrested in June 2007 for shoplifting at a shopping mall near her home in Kingstown, Rhode Island. The police report listed five items worth $67 she allegedly stole from an Old Navy store.

She paid restitution into a crime victims fund and performed community service. Afterward, a judge dismissed the case. Her former attorney described the case as a common lapse of judgment among teenaged shoplifters.

When she started at Suffolk University as a freshman in 2007, her first friends described her as a social butterfly who was fun to have around. She met Tamerlan in a nightclub not long after she started working toward a major in communications. Her friends started noticing gradual changes in Katherine as she hung around with Tamerlan more often.

They dated only sporadically at first but more often as she seemed to fall under the influence of the flashy-dressing boxer. Her friends said he sometimes treated her disrespectfully, even calling her a "slut," but she stayed with him. While still in college, she converted to Islam, began wearing the hijab style of dress of Muslim women and changed her name to Karima.

Tamerlan's boxer friends said he talked happily about her occasionally and said he planned to propose to her.

During her senior year, she became pregnant by Tamerlan, prompting her to drop out of school. They married on June 21, 2011, in a 15-minute ceremony with two witnesses on the third floor of Dorchester's Masjid Al Quran mosque.

The mosque's imam who performed the ceremony described it as just one more wedding. He led them through the vows, instructed them on being faithful to the Creator and to each other. She wore a scarf and seemed happy.

The wedding certificate listed his occupation as "driver" and hers as "student."

After moving into her husband's Cambridge apartment, the newly rechristened Karima Tsarnaeva worked long hours as a home health aide, sometimes more than 70 hours per week. Tamerlan worked several short-term jobs but mostly stayed at home taking care of their daughter. The couple supplemented their income with food stamps and public assistance.

Their friends described her as quiet and submissive around her domineering husband but friendlier and warmer when he was not present. Neighbors said they heard them arguing loudly at times.

Her new lifestyle was much different from the life of New England privilege provided by her parents. Both her father and grandfather were Yale graduates. Katherine stayed at the couple's Cambridge home while her husband traveled to Russia for six months shortly before the Boston Marathon bombings. She considered following her husband to Russia for the opportunity to learn a new language and culture.

After the bombings, police came to their home searching for her. She was in the apartment with neighbors. Police ordered them all to leave. Katherine was dressed in black. She tried to borrow a cellphone from a neighbor but a police officer grabbed it away from her.

As photographs of her flashed around the country after the bombings, part of the public fascination with Katherine was her conversion to Islam and her Muslim style of dress.

"Yes, the hijab, the scarlet letter of doom," wrote Muslim journalist Deanna Othman in a Huffington Post essay. Tamerlan's widow "provides a spectacle for the public to shake their heads at because she is a tragic character, and her tragic flaw is her conversion to the Muslim faith."

She moved back to her parents' Rhode Island home after her husband died. Her parents issued a statement saying their "daughter has lost her husband today, the father of her child. We cannot begin to comprehend how this horrible tragedy occurred. In the aftermath of the Patriots Day horror, we know that we never really knew Tamerlan Tsarnaev. Our hearts are sickened by the knowledge of the horror he has inflicted."

Any criminal evidence against her is sketchy and circumstantial. The FBI found bomb-making instructions taken from a magazine on her computer but it is uncertain who downloaded it. Explosive residue was found in the home she shared with Tamerlan, but there is no proof it came from Katherine or that she knew about it.

She told FBI interrogators that she saw her husband the day before the bombing but was flabbergasted to learn of his involvement.

Police were skeptical of Tamerlan's wife, particularly after Dzhokhar told them he and his brother assembled the bombs in the Cambridge apartment shared by Katherine. In addition, police said she accompanied Tamerlan to Macy's department store two months before the marathon to purchase the pressure cookers that were used as casings for the bombs.

However, her DNA did not match any human samples found on the bombs.

She admitted sending a text message to her husband after police published his name and photograph. She refused to disclose what it said. Police found copies of Inspire magazine on her computer but could not prove she downloaded them.

Her attorneys issued a statement in late April saying the bombings "caused profound distress and sorrow to Katie and her family." The statement added, "the reports of involvement by her husband and brother-in-law came as an absolute shock to them all."

After Tamerlan died, she returned to using her maiden name. She also refused to take custody of Tamerlan's remains.

Even burying Tamerlan's battered body became a major struggle. The body remained unclaimed in a morgue for two weeks before a Worcester funeral home volunteered to help with the funeral arrangements.

Protesters from the local community said they did not want

a terrorist buried near them. Instead, they said the body should be sent back to Russia. One protester held a sign that said, "Bury the garbage in the landfill." Cambridge's city manager said he would not allow burial in his community because of public outrage toward the Tsarnaevs.

The issue was resolved when an interfaith coalition arranged burial at a Muslim cemetery at rural Doswell, Virginia. The group said it was not motivated by politics, only a humanitarian effort.

The burial was done quietly, unannounced, in an unmarked grave.

The rechristened Katherine Russell remarried less than two years after Tamerlan's death.

FRIENDS FOREVER

FRIENDSHIP WITH THE affable Dzhokhar became an unfortunate life-changing event for four of his fellow college students and his older sister, Alina.

Dias Kadyrbayev, Azamat Tazhayakov and Robel Phillipos entered the University of Massachusetts at Dartmouth along with Dzhokhar in the fall of 2011. Their ability to speak Russian became the common bond that drew the teenagers together. Phillipos had attended high school with Dzhokhar.

Kadyrbayev and Tazhayakov became Dzhokhar's dormitory roommates. When they later leased an apartment in New Bedford, Dzhokhar often visited them while keeping his own dorm room on campus.

When police published the still-unidentified suspects' photos on television after the bombings, his three Russian-speaking friends wanted to help. Unfortunately for them, their definition of help meant going to Dzhokhar's dorm room, retrieving his backpack that contained his laptop computer and fireworks and dumping them in a landfill outside New Bedford.

Police took the men into custody on April 18 on charges they violated their student visas. Initially, they denied knowing anything about the bombings or taking anything out of Dzhokhar's dorm room.

They were released after the initial questioning but re-arrested on April 20 as police found out more about their association with Dzhokhar.

Later, they admitted taking the backpack and laptop. Police recovered them from the landfill on April 26. The fireworks inside the backpack were the same kind used to make the bombs detonated at the marathon.

Dzhokhar's friends suddenly became much more than casual observers. They were charged with obstruction of justice and conspiracy.

Kadyrbayev listened quietly as a prosecutor read a statement of allegations against the 20-year-old former college student at a hearing in Boston. He pleaded guilty to obstruction of justice and conspiracy to obstruct justice.

"Is that all true," U.S. District Judge Douglas Woodlock asked Kadyrbayev.

"Yes," he replied.

Prosecutors agreed to ask for no more than a seven-year prison sentence for Kadyrbayev in exchange for his guilty plea instead of the maximum 25 years allowed under the law.

His attorney released a statement saying his client was "a young man, just 19 years old at the time, who made a terrible error in judgment for which he has paid dearly."

A jury found Tazhayakov guilty of being a co-conspirator with Kadyrbayev in trying to destroy evidence.

His defense attorney tried to portray Tazhayakov as a victim of heated politics who prosecutors wanted to convict under the theory of "guilt by association."

"If you want to find a conspiracy, you probably can because you're letting the enormity of what happened in this town affect you," attorney Matthew Myers told the jury during closing arguments. "The reality is, college kids think differently."

Jurors interviewed after the verdict said evidence Tazhayakov participated in the decision to throw the backpack into the trash dumpster were too incriminating to overlook.

Phillipos was convicted of lying to the FBI.

In a similar way, actions by Alina Tsarnaeva might have been overlooked at another time and in another circumstance if not for the publicity surrounding her family after the bombings.

She was arrested on charges of misdemeanor aggravated harassment after allegedly making a bomb threat to a romantic rival. Her boyfriend had a child by the woman who said Tsarnaeva threatened her.

Although the then 24-year-old turned herself in to New York City police on Aug. 27, she denied threatening anyone. She lived nearby in North Bergen, New Jersey.

She allegedly told the rival during a telephone conversation, "I know people that can put a bomb where you live."

Her attorney claimed she was prosecuted because of her brothers. She was released from police custody while wearing the traditional Muslim women's gown and headscarf after posting $5,000 bail.

CONGRESS DEMANDS ANSWERS

THREE WEEKS AFTER Tamerlan died and Dzhokhar was arrested, Congress demanded answers at a Capitol Hill hearing about how the alleged bombers slipped through their multi-billion dollar anti-terrorism network. It would be the first of several congressional hearings over the next year that mentioned the marathon bombings.

"To put it bluntly, our homeland defense system failed in Boston," former Senator Joe Lieberman, an Independent from Connecticut, said in a May 9 statement during a House Homeland Security Committee hearing.

Lieberman was one of the political leaders who designed the U.S. Department of Homeland Security after the September 11 attacks.

The May 9 congressional hearing was the first of four on lessons to be learned from the marathon bombings. Unlike the white-knuckled outrage that followed the September 11, 2001 attacks, congressmen were more concerned than scandalized.

"Though it would not have been easy, it was possible to prevent the terrorist attacks in Boston," Lieberman said.

He was particularly distressed by what he said was a lack of information-sharing between agencies that might have identified the Tsarnaevs as high-level terrorist risks. Congress also blamed faulty information-sharing between the FBI and other agencies as a big factor for failing to stop the September 11 attacks.

The FBI had a chance to stop Tamerlan Tsarnaev when Russian intelligence agencies notified them he was a suspected Muslim extremist years earlier but missed the opportunity, Lieberman said.

"Why didn't the [Department of Homeland Security] notify the FBI and the Boston JTTF [Joint Terrorism Task Force] when its system pinged that Tamerlan Tsarnaev had left America for Russia on his way to Dagestan," Lieberman asked.

Tamerlan was spotted setting the bombs in Boston less than a year after he returned from Dagestan, where Russian police said he met with terrorists.

"I'm agitated by why nobody was particularly looking for the name Tamerlan Tsarnaev by the time he came back," Lieberman said. "Someone should have been on him."

Taking some of the heat was Boston Police Commissioner Ed Davis, who told the congressmen more surveillance cameras might be part of the answer.

"I strongly support the enhanced ability to monitor public places," Davis said. "This monitoring ... violates no constitutionally protected rights but gives police the ability to investigate and effectively prosecute. Images from cameras do not lie. They do not forget."

More camera surveillance has become a hot issue for civil liberties groups, such as the American Civil Liberties Union. They warn that the zeal to protect the United States could spill over into police-state invasions of privacy.

Davis acknowledged the risks to privacy when he said in his statement, "I do not endorse actions that move Boston and our nation into a police state mentality, with surveillance cameras attached to every light pole in the city."

He seemed to ask for understanding of how Boston police are confronting the dilemma when he said the marathon bombings created "the most complex crime scene we ever processed in the city."

Rep. Michael McCaul, a Texas Republican, asked, "Were you aware of the Russian intelligence warning?"

Davis responded that he was "not in fact informed of that particular development." He added, "We would have liked to know."

McCaul was least forgiving of the Homeland Security Department. "The whole point of the fusion centers and the Joint Terrorism Task Forces is to share information," he said. "The whole idea of information not shared defies why we even have a Homeland Security Department in the first place."

The May 9 hearing was followed by two more hearings in the House and Senate on July 10. That time, the FBI felt the brunt of the lawmakers' anger.

House Homeland Security Committee Chairman McCaul accused the FBI of withholding information requested by members of Congress. They demanded to know what the FBI knew about the Tsarnaevs before the marathon bombings.

Not only did the FBI decline to turn over the information, the agency also did not send anyone to testify at the congressional hearings.

"It is this committee's responsibility to find out how we did not see it coming," said McCaul, a Texas Republican. "We are going to find out what happened, what went wrong and how to fix it."

The FBI did respond to the committee after the hearing. The agency issued a statement saying it did not want to comment during an ongoing investigation to "protect the integrity of the judicial process."

FBI spokesman Paul Bresson said, "This involves ensuring both the government's ability to conduct a successful prosecution as well as protecting the rights of all parties involved, including the victims, their families and the defendant, who, as it turns out, has a court appearance on the same day as this hearing."

For the same reasons, the FBI declined to comment on questions for this report.

Additional criticism came from the Senate Homeland Security and Governmental Affairs Committee hearing.

Kurt N. Schwartz, a Massachusetts public safety official, testified the FBI failed to tell State Police that Tamerlan Tsarnaev had been investigated by the agency.

Boston Police Commissioner Davis suggested the Justice Department terrorism task forces run by the FBI should have a mission statement requiring them to share threat information with local police.

His information-sharing suggestion won agreement from members of the congressional committee and Michael Leiter, former head of the National Counterterrorism Center.

But Leiter added that task force rules requiring secrecy on national security threats sometimes make information-sharing difficult.

Davis had nicer comments about the FBI for their cooperation after the marathon bombings. The senators and witnesses also praised emergency responders.

"'Boston Strong' was no accident," said Richard Serino, a Federal Emergency Management Agency deputy administrator. "It was years of planning, years of training, years of purchasing the right equipment for the right people at the right time, and it saved lives."

Arthur L. Kellermann, a RAND Corporation analyst and physician, said Boston's emergency personnel developed some of their response strategy from studying how terrorist attacks in Madrid, London and elsewhere were handled.

"Boston's responders were both lucky and good, that's why so many victims survived," Kellermann testified. "They were prepared to do a great job ... Everyone knew what to do. That's how disaster plans work."

He cautioned that there was no guarantee Boston's well-managed emergency response could be copied in other communities.

"The number of trauma patients any one hospital got was very manageable," Kellermann said. "We cannot put seven trauma centers in every American city. Massachusetts can barely afford it. Our nation can't afford it."

In most other cities, the death toll from the bombings would have been higher, he said.

Interviews for this report with Boston area police departments generally showed satisfaction with their response to the marathon bombings.

Daniel Riviello, spokesman for the Cambridge Police Department, said, "We believe that our officers and our counterparts at other agencies were well-trained and prepared to handle these events."

Local police are trying to learn what more they could do in similar situations in the future, he said. "We are taking this as an opportunity to review the events with our department, take another look at our training and make modifications if necessary," Riviello said.

Massachusetts Bay Transportation Authority Police Chief Paul MacMillan said, "We review each incident, as we will this one, and make any adjustments or changes as we feel appropriate to better protect the passengers of the MBTA. If we feel any are necessary, we would not comment on the specifics of those changes."

Members of Congress saw the warning signs about homegrown terrorism years earlier and sought answers on how to stop incidents such as the marathon bombings. Each time, they ran into complaints about ethnic stereotyping of Muslims.

A March 10, 2011 hearing of the House Homeland Security Committee showed deep divisions among the committee members. Republicans were concerned that Muslims did not obey U.S. laws and Democrats warned against trampling the rights of followers of Islam.

Equally deep divisions appeared among members of the Islamic community who testified at the hearing.

Melvin Bledsoe, a Memphis businessman, told Congress about his son, who converted to Islam in college and traveled to Yemen, where he became "trained and programmed" to kill, his father said. He later opened fire on a military recruiting center in Little Rock, Ark., where one soldier was killed and another wounded.

"Our children are in danger," Bledsoe said as he warned about Islamic extremism.

Representative Keith Ellison, a Muslim, wept as he told about Mohammed Salman Hamdani, a volunteer medical technician in New York who tried to help victims after the first World Trade Center tower collapsed during the Sept. 11, 2001 terrorist attack. He was killed when the other tower collapsed.

As the investigation of the attack began, his sudden disappearance raised alarms among investigators about whether he was involved in the plot. The suspicions were erased only after the 23-year-old Hamdani's body was recovered from the debris.

Like most of the congressional hearings on homegrown terrorism, the hearing ended there: Great concern about extremists, no definitive solutions and many warnings about trampling the rights of innocent Muslims.

U.S. lawmakers' most successful effort against terrorism was the USA Patriot Act, which broadened the authority of federal agencies to conduct surveillance and loosened privacy restrictions for private citizens.

President George W. Bush signed it into law on Oct. 26, 2001, while smoke still wafted from the debris of New York's World Trade Center. Other provisions of the law strengthened anti-money laundering measures to prevent terrorists from hiding their income sources. It also cracked down on illegal immigration and instituted new information-sharing strategies among law enforcement agencies.

Congress reauthorized the USA Patriot Act in 2005 but with more restrictions on electronic surveillance to respond to complaints from civil liberties groups.

Other legislation, such as the Violent Radicalization and Homegrown Terrorism Prevention Act of 2007, was criticized for being too controversial, too vague and too open-ended in the goals it sought.

The proposed law, introduced in the House by Rep. Jane Harman, a California Democrat, would set up a national commission on homegrown terrorism, establish a center to study violent radicalization and seek cooperation with other nations to stop it.

The bill passed in the House in April 2007 but never reached a vote in the Senate, where it appears to have died. Former presidential candidate and congressman Dennis Kucinich called it a "thought crime bill" and "unconstitutional."

But even members of Congress who led the U.S. legislative campaign to combat terrorism grew increasingly skeptical of their own efforts as Islamic radicals became increasingly violent.

During a Sept. 17, 2014 House Homeland Security hearing, McCaul said, "The ideological struggle against violent Islamist extremists is taking place not just overseas, but also here at home. There have been more than 70 homegrown violent jihadist plots or attacks in the United States since 9/11."

Most of the plots were stopped by law enforcement but the threat is ongoing, he said.

"Many of the suspects were radicalized, at least in part, by online Islamist propaganda, including the Boston Marathon bombers..." McCaul said.

FBI Director James Comey added, "These are the homegrown violent extremists that we worry about, who can get all the poison they need and the training they need to kill Americans, and in a way that's very hard for us to spot between the time they emerge from their basements and maybe kill innocent Americans."

HOMEGROWN TERRORISM TAKES ROOT

IT WOULD BE hard to find accused Islamic extremists who fit the mold of homegrown terrorists better than the Tsarnaev brothers.

Profiles compiled by the FBI, the Congressional Research Service, private psychologists and the New York City Police Department found common factors that describe Tamerlan Tsarnaev almost perfectly.

Typically, terrorists are male Muslims, less than 35 years old, citizens of Western countries where they are local residents and the children of immigrants. They come from middle-class backgrounds and are reasonably well educated, often university students.

They also tend to be recent converts to Islam who were not originally devout Muslims. They usually have little criminal history.

The alleged Boston Marathon bombers not only fit the profile of the most successful terrorists but also the ones most vexing for the FBI: lone wolves. Lone wolves refer to activists who commit violence to support a group or ideology, but they do it alone, without help and with no command structure to direct them.

They have included Egyptian-American Hesham Mohamed Hadayet, who shot randomly at an El Al ticket stand on July 4, 2002, killing two people. Another was Muslim American Naveed Afzal Haq, who shot and killed one woman and injured five other persons July 28, 2006, at the Seattle Jewish Federation. On June 1, 2009, American Islamist convert Abdulhakim Majahid Muhammad killed one solider and wounded a second when he shot them at a Little Rock, Ark., military recruiting station.

The most deadly lone wolf in recent years was Nidal Malik Hasan, who killed 13 people and injured 30 when he shot them at Fort Hood, Texas, on Nov. 5, 2009.

Most terrorism arises from international organizations whose leaders can be tracked and whose orders often are overheard by informants. Their plots most commonly are found in threat assessments from the FBI and U.S. military.

Lone wolves seem to come out of nowhere with no warning about when and where they might attack.

Lone wolves who reside in the countries they attack are the most deadly of all. They have no barriers to entering the countries. They are familiar with the society and have no difficulty communicating with the native population. They also know which targets would be most valuable and most easily attacked.

Often, they are new recruits or converts to Islam who have not yet aroused enough suspicion to be tracked by law enforcement agencies. Their attacks usually are low-cost operations involving only a few guns or crude, homemade bombs, which makes them even more attractive for a decentralized organization like al Qaeda.

Not all of the homegrown terrorism attacks are perpetrated by Muslims. Others have included the 1995 Oklahoma City bombing by Timothy McVeigh that killed 168 people and the

1996 Summer Olympics bombing in Atlanta by anti-abortion and anti-gay fundamentalist Eric Rudolph.

However, the FBI reports that terrorist plots by Islamic extremists are increasing as al Qaeda's leadership switches strategies to encourage more privately-sponsored acts of violence. Between Sept. 11, 2001, and May 2009, the FBI reported it made arrests in 21 terrorist plots inspired by Islamic extremists. By comparison, 22 Islamic-inspired plots resulted in arrests between May 2009 and November 2010.

The strategy shift was mentioned by American-born al Qaeda spokesman Adam Gadahn in a June 2011 English language video message to fellow Islamic extremists. He encouraged lone wolf attacks by saying, "Let's take America for example. America is absolutely awash with easily obtainable firearms. You can go down to a gun show at the local convention center and come away with a fully automatic assault rifle, without a background check, and most likely without having to show an identification card. So what are you waiting for?"

Gadahn suggests "targeting major institutions" while a clip played on his video showing the logos of corporations such as Exxon, Merrill Lynch and Bank of America. He also suggested targeting "influential public figures."

The Congressional Research Service, a research agency for Congress, defined homegrown terrorism as "terrorist activity or plots perpetuated within the United States or abroad by American citizens, permanent legal residents or visitors radicalized largely within the United States."

Former CIA Director Michael Hayden called homegrown terrorism one of the most serious threats Americans face as a nation.

"How do you build a security structure that guards you against American citizens who are beginning to change in their thinking up to a point where they become a threat to the security of other Americans," Hayden asked during a 2010 interview on

CNN. "That's a devil of a problem."

The Bipartisan Policy Center, a public policy foundation, noted the threat of homegrown terrorism in its Sept. 10, 2010 report entitled Assessing the Terrorist Threat.

"As the ranks of U.S. recruits have grown, the new frontlines have become the streets of Bridgeport, Denver, Minneapolis and other big and small communities across America," the report said.

Much of the battle over homegrown terrorism is wrapped up in a struggle to win the minds of sympathizers. The Internet plays a key role.

The FBI estimates there are 10,000 active websites worldwide that support terrorist activities. About 80 percent of them are accessible through U.S. computer servers.

Osama bin-Laden once said that 90 percent of his battle is fought through the media. Al Qaeda's biggest year for its media battle was in 2007, when its video production teams released nearly 100 tapes over the Internet.

One of the early Islamic extremist websites was launched in 2003 by Abu Musab al-Zarqawi, the leader of al Qaeda in Iraq, who used it to post videos of beheadings.

Since then, the Internet's role for militant extremists has grown to include chat rooms and message boards where they can communicate anonymously. Their virtual network communities have provided a means to make plans, recruit members and exchange information on weapons and targets.

A centerpiece of Islamic extremist attention is the online magazine Inspire. It is published by al Qaeda in the Arabian Peninsula and reportedly edited by U.S. citizen Samir Khan. The writing style of the English-language magazine reflects American speech and phrasing.

Part of the magazine gives tips on how to carry out attacks, such as with homemade bombs or just running over Islamic enemies in cars. Other articles encourage jihad — or holy war —

by Western sympathizers of Islam. One message from al Qaeda in the Arabian Peninsula leader Nasir al-Wahayshi says western jihadists should try "to acquire weapons and learn methods of war. They are living in a place where they can cause great harm to the enemy and where they can support the Messenger of Allah...

"The means of harming them are many so seek assistance from Allah and do not be weak and you will find a way."

The government investigation of the Boston Marathon bombings revealed that the Internet might have helped the Tsarnaev brothers learn to prepare their bombs.

According to the federal indictment against him, Dzhokhar Tsarnaev downloaded propaganda from extremist Islamic web sites that advised Muslims to resist governments that invade Arab countries. Technical details about how to build the bombs came from Volume 1 of the radical Islamist online magazine Inspire, investigators said.

Other times, Inspire has advised Western jihadists about what to expect when they travel to training camps in Yemen or other parts of the Middle East. Articles have suggested learning the local language and bringing a friend to decrease loneliness in the new foreign surroundings.

U.S. law enforcement agencies have responded by trying to enlist public support for their anti-terrorist efforts, such as with their "If you see something, say something" campaign that encourages private citizens to report suspicious activity.

Increasingly, the enemy they seek to reveal can be traced to the United States rather than some far-off Middle Eastern country. In fact, some Americans have ascended to leadership roles in al Qaeda and other terrorist organizations.

"Al Qaeda and its Pakistani, Somali and Yemeni allies arguably have been able to accomplish the unthinkable — establishing at least an embryonic terrorist recruitment, radicalization and operational infrastructure in the United

States with effects both at home and abroad," according to the Bipartisan Policy Center's report. "And, by working through its local allies, the group has now allowed them to co-opt American citizens in the broader global al Qaeda battlefield."

They include Anwar al-Awlaki, David Headley and Adam Gadahn. Awlaki, who was born in New Mexico, was a Muslim cleric who led al Qaeda's recruiting efforts. He is believed to have communicated with three of the September 11 hijackers. He also made masterful use of the Internet to advocate for Islam and for violence against Muslim enemies. He was killed in a U.S. airstrike on Sept. 30, 2011, in Yemen.

Washington, D.C.-born David Headley helped Islamic militants identify targets for the 2008 attacks in Mumbai. He also conspired to attack the headquarters of a Copenhagen newspaper that published cartoons insulting to the prophet Mohammad. Headley faces life in U.S. federal prison after pleading guilty to terrorism-related charges.

Adam Gadahn, born Adam Pearlman in Oregon, was a spokesman, senior operative and advisor for al Qaeda before he was killed by a U.S. counterterrorism strike in January 2015. He has appeared in several al Qaeda videos criticizing the United States and is believed to have organized Osama bin Laden's 2007 video. He was under indictment by a federal court in California for treason and aiding the enemy. On the fourth anniversary of the September 11 attacks, he broadcast a video replayed on ABC News that warned of future terrorist acts, similar to train and bus bombings in London and Madrid. "Yesterday, London and Madrid," he said. "Tomorrow, Los Angeles and Melbourne, God willing. At this time, don't count on us demonstrating restraint or compassion."

The Bipartisan Policy Center report says Americans are taking bigger roles in terrorist threats.

"A key shift in the threat to the homeland since around the time President Barack Obama took office is the increasing

'Americanization' of the leadership of al Qaeda and aligned groups, and their larger numbers of Americans attaching themselves to these groups," the report says.

The report predicts a bigger shift of terrorism toward "soft" targets that are only thinly protected against violence. Attacks on military targets, such as battleships and Army bases, have caused only small damage.

Soft targets typically refer to places that consist mostly of civilians and produce broad economic damage, as well as widespread publicity. Examples include civil aviation and American hotels. Another one could be the Boston Marathon.

With terrorism's many sources and forms, police describe preventing it as being as elusive as trying to swat a flea with your hand. Investigating crimes already committed provides minimal protection against future attacks, according to the Congressional Research Service's January 2013 report, "American Jihadist Terrorism: Combating a Complex Threat."

Instead, the FBI and other agencies seek to be preventive. "A major challenge for law enforcement is gauging how quickly and at what point individuals move from radicalized beliefs to violence so that a terrorist plot can be detected and disrupted," the report says.

A top tool for federal investigators is assessments that weigh risk factors to discover the most likely threats. Although they help with predictions, they also create huge controversy.

In most cases, police need "probable cause" to seek a warrant or make an arrest that might stop further crime. Probable cause means they have tangible evidence showing the persons being investigated are engaged in criminal activity.

For terrorism, they cannot wait until a crime is committed because of the devastation it creates. As a result, people only suspected of sympathizing with terrorists could fall under investigation with the new federal guidelines.

"The new guidelines have, however, generated some

controversy among civil libertarians," the Congressional Research Service report says.

Another prevention method used by the FBI involves monitoring Internet and social networking sites that might be visited by extremists. The USA Patriot Act authorizes the FBI to go beyond watching the sites to include tracing email messages and previous Internet use of suspects. Often, they are searching for evidence that extremists might have linked with other extremists.

Evidence the FBI compiled on Internet or email use has been mentioned in at least 28 criminal complaints or indictments against suspected jihadists since the September 11 attacks.

However, lone wolves are not as easily identified by assessments and Internet communications as terrorists operating in an international network. The FBI has been trying to shift some of the investigation to local law enforcement agencies that are closely connected to communities where terrorists might arise.

The Justice Department has organized Joint Terrorism Task Forces to coordinate investigations between state and federal police. Some states and large cities have set up their own "fusion centers" to share information with federal agencies. Their information-sharing program is called the Nationwide Suspicious Activity Report Initiative.

Their tactics often include what they call the "Al Capone" approach to stopping terrorists. Because they will not risk waiting for a large-scale terrorist attack, they try to arrest the suspects on lesser charges, such as immigration law violations.

Similar tactics have been used previously against mafia bosses, corrupt public officials and white collar criminals. They often hide their bigger crimes by working through co-conspirators or by intimidating witnesses, similar to the way Al Capone's accusers might mysteriously and suddenly disappear.

The FBI also has used the "agent provocateur" strategy,

more commonly known as sting operations. Undercover agents will befriend suspects with pledges to help them commit terrorist attacks.

One of the sting operations stopped a Moroccan man who told undercover FBI agents he hoped to kill 30 people at the U.S. Capitol building in a Feb. 17, 2012 suicide attack.

He was carrying a MAC-10 gun and a vest he believed was packed with explosives and nails. They were given to him by an FBI agent posing as an al Qaeda operative who had disabled both the gun and the explosives without telling the attacker, Amine El Khalifi.

He had been living in Alexandria, Va., and attending a local mosque. An informer who witnessed El Khalifi's statements sympathizing with Islamic jihad reported him to the FBI.

Undercover agents befriended him before arresting him in a parking lot only a short walk from the Capitol.

The case demonstrated the effectiveness of winning the trust and cooperation of the American Muslim community. Since the September 11 attacks, the FBI has actively sought help from the Muslim, Arab and Sikh communities to stop terrorism, the Congressional Research Service reported. The cooperative efforts are modeled on community policing tactics developed in the 1990s. They rely on "watch groups" of private citizens who agree to monitor high crime areas and activities in their neighborhoods for suspicious behavior that they report to police.

Although public officials generally support enlisting Muslim community support, the Congressional Research Service says building the trust for them is "difficult."

"Especially challenging are law enforcement activities perceived by community members to be unfairly targeting law-abiding citizens or infringing on speech, religion, assembly or due process rights," the Congressional Research Service report said.

Confidential informants helped police in at least 33 cases of suspected terrorism since the September 11 attacks. Therein lies another controversy for law enforcement: the betrayal of trust inherent in using informants might outrage jihadists into further violence.

The congressional agency's report asks, "Is the impact of that tactic counterproductive in the long run, or is it necessary, short-term collateral damage?"

THE ROGUES GALLERY

SENATOR MARCO RUBIO, a Florida Republican who serves on the Senate Intelligence Committee, sounded the alarm about lone wolf terrorists days after the marathon bombings when he told reporters, "This is a new element of terrorism that we have to face in our country. We need to be prepared for Boston-type attacks, not just 9/11-type attacks."

The following is a run-down of Islamic lone wolf terrorists in the United States.

Ali Hassan Abu Kamal fired randomly with a handgun at visitors to the Empire State Building's observation deck in New York City on Feb. 23, 1997. He killed one person, wounded six others then committed suicide with a gunshot to his head.

Initial reports varied on his motives. Police said they found notes from Abu Kamal showing outrage over political tensions between Israel and Palestinians. Abu Kamal was a 69-year-old retired Palestinian teacher who moved to New York in 1996 after a successful career.

However, his wife said Abu Kamal was upset over a business failure. She said two business partners swindled him out of about $300,000 of his money, making him suicidal.

"My husband is not a terrorist, he was just hopeless," Fathiya Abu Kamal said in a CNN report. "He was aged, he had nothing to do with politics or terrorism or crime."

Ten years later, Abu Kamal's daughter, Linda, told a different story about his motives. She said her father wanted to punish the United States, Britain and France for supporting Israel. She admitted that her mother had not told the truth.

"A Palestinian Authority official advised us to say the attack was not for political reasons because that would harm the peace agreement with Israel," according to a 2007 New York Daily News report quoting Abu Kamal's daughter. "[Kamal's] goal was patriotic. He wanted to take revenge from the Americans, the British, the French and the Israelis ... He wrote that after he raised his children and made sure that his family was all right, he decided to avenge in the highest building in America to make sure they get his message."

Before Abu Kamal started shooting during the Empire State Building attack, he mumbled something about Egypt, then shouted "Are you from Egypt?" Police were uncertain why he shouted the question but said it might have been to identify and to spare fellow Arabs from his attack.

The only victim who died was 27-year-old Christoffer Burmeister, a Danish musician living in New York. His fellow band member, Matthew Gross, was critically wounded.

He used a .380-caliber Beretta handgun that he had purchased in Florida after giving a fake local address for his home. The address was the hotel where he was staying. His easy access to the gun purchase prompted outrage in New York over loose gun control laws.

Hesham Mohammed Hadayet killed two people and injured four when he fired at strangers at an El Al ticket stand at Los Angeles International Airport on July 4, 2002.

Hadayet was a 41-year-old Egyptian citizen who arrived in the United States in 1992 on a tourist visa. He received permission to stay from U.S. immigration officials after claiming refugee status. Returning to his homeland could have subjected him to political reprisal because he was a member of the Muslim Brotherhood, he said.

At that point, he sank into a non-descript lifestyle as a resident of Irvine, Calif. His wife helped him obtain a green card through a U.S. Immigration and Naturalization Service lottery that allowed him to start a business as a limousine driver. He lived with his wife and two sons, 8 years old and 11 years old, in a condominium.

All of it changed one Thursday morning when Hadayet walked up to the ticket counter of the Israeli national airline at Los Angeles International Airport. He suddenly pulled out two handguns and began firing. The first victim was Victoria Hen, a 25-year-old flight attendant, who was standing behind the ticket counter. She died from a gunshot wound to her chest.

Next, Hadayet began firing at some of the 90 passengers standing in line. They already had started huddling when he shot the flight attendant. The next fatality was 46-year-old passenger Yaakov Aminov. Four other bystanders were injured.

After Hadayet fired 10 shots, an unarmed El Al security guard knocked him down. Hadayet stabbed a second security officer who ran to the scene. Nevertheless, the second officer was able to pull his gun and kill Hadayet by shooting him in the abdomen.

An FBI investigation concluded that Hadayet acted alone under a belief that his attack could pressure U.S. lawmakers to adopt policies favoring Palestinians.

Other factors influencing his irrational attack included business failure for his limousine service, a failing marriage and loneliness on his birthday — the same day of his attack at the airport.

Mohammed Reza Taheri-azar left no doubt about his intentions when he ran into a crowd of people at the University of North Carolina at Chapel Hill in a sport utility vehicle.

He told police he wanted to "punish" the United States government and to "avenge the deaths of Muslims worldwide."

Nine people were injured but none died when Taheri-azar drove his rented 2006 Jeep Grand Cherokee into a campus courtyard known locally as the Pit. It was a popular gathering place surrounded by libraries, the student center and a bookstore.

Witnesses estimated his speed at 40 mph to 45 mph as he hit nine pedestrians. Six were treated at a hospital and released. Three others declined treatment.

Although the amount of damage and injury was relatively small, the message was clear: "I was aiming to follow in the footsteps of one of my role models, Mohamed Atta, one of the 9/11 hijackers, who obtained a doctorate degree," Taheri-azar wrote in a letter he left for police in his apartment.

Taheri-azar, who was born in Iran, graduated from the University of North Carolina at Chapel Hill only three months before the attack. Police later found his blue graduation gown in a closet in his apartment.

Minutes after the attack, he called a police dispatcher to turn himself in. During a March 6, 2006 Orange County Superior Court pre-trial hearing, he said he preferred to defend himself, which would include invoking the law of Allah.

On Aug. 26, 2008, he was sentenced to 26-to-33 years in prison for two counts of attempted murder.

Local Muslim leaders condemned Taheri-azar for linking his attack to the Koran.

Naveed Afzal Haq shouted, "I am a Muslim American angry at Israel," as he shot people at the Seattle Jewish Federation building during a July 28, 2006 attack. One woman was killed and five others injured.

Haq, who has Pakistani ancestry and whose father is a prominent Muslim American leader, was 33 years old when he grabbed a 13-year-old girl and held a gun to her back. He allegedly ordered her to dial the intercom and ask to be buzzed inside the building.

As he entered the building, he started shooting. Pamela Waechter was killed and Layla Bush critically injured. Four other women suffered lesser injuries.

He spoke with police dispatchers while the confrontation continued. "These are Jews and I'm tired of getting pushed around and our people getting pushed around by the situation in the Middle East," he reportedly said. He demanded the United States withdraw its military from Iraq.

He agreed to surrender after he calmed down, then walked out of the building with his hands on his head. The nine charges against him included murder and a hate crime.

During the first trial, the jury was unable to reach a unanimous verdict. During a second trial, the jury rejected Haq's insanity defense based on his bipolar disorder. He was convicted on all counts, including first-degree murder on Dec. 15, 2009. He was sentenced to life in prison plus 120 years.

Abdulhakim Mujahid Muhammad brought all the zeal of a convert to his June 1, 2009 attack on the Little Rock, Ark., military recruiting station. One young Army private was killed and a second wounded as he fired into them with a Soviet semi-automatic SKS rifle during a drive-by shooting.

Terrorism experts who commented on the high-profile case noted how closely the attack fit the profile for lone wolf terrorists, namely a young assailant motivated by ideology and religion hitting a target associated with the United States.

The father of Private William Andrew Long, 23, who was smoking a cigarette outside the recruiting station when he was shot and killed, said, "They weren't on the battlefield, but apparently the battlefield's here."

Muhammad was born Carlos Leon Bledsoe on July 9, 1985, in Memphis, Tenn., to the owner of a charter bus company. He was raised a Baptist and considered a happy child.

He converted to Islam a year after graduating from high

school, while he attended Tennessee State University in Nashville. He later reportedly said, "I've loved jihad ever since I became a Muslim."

He prayed often at the Islamic Center of Nashville. In 2007, without having graduated from college, he traveled to Yemen for a 16-month stay, where he taught English and learned to speak Arabic. He married a Yemeni elementary school teacher in 2008.

In his handwritten letters after he was arrested, Muhammad said people in Yemen who helped set him up there also asked him to attack targets in the United States. His apparent willingness to help them prompted extremists to arrange explosives training for him in Somalia. The training was supposed to focus on car bombs.

Muhammad never completed his training. Instead, Yemeni police who stopped him during a routine traffic check on Nov. 14, 2008, arrested him for overstaying his visa.

A letter he wrote to the Memphis Commercial Appeal newspaper in 2010 said, "Had I got this training my story would have ended a lot differently than it's going to end now. My drive-by would have been a drive-in, with no one escaping the aftermath."

Muhammad was deported back to the United States after two months of imprisonment in Yemen. While he was imprisoned, he said he started his plan for jihad against the United States. His lawyer later said Islamic fundamentalists radicalized him in jail.

He moved in with his parents after returning to the United States in January 2009. In April, he moved to Little Rock, Ark., where he worked out of the local office of his father's business as a tour bus driver.

The FBI's Joint Terrorism Task Force investigated Muhammad, including a visit to Columbus, Ohio, where he was suspected of associating with Somali Americans who were preparing for jihad.

He said in letters to the Commercial Appeal that he had taken measures to conceal his activities even while he stockpiled second-hand guns and ammunition and practiced target shooting.

He also acknowledged his first plan to kill rabbis and attack Jewish organizations did not go well for him. Muhammad started his personal jihad by driving to Nashville, where he threw a Molotov cocktail at a rabbi's house. The Molotov cocktail did not ignite.

He then drove to an Army recruiting center in Florence, Kentucky with plans to shoot soldiers. The Florence recruiting center was closed. However, the Little Rock recruiting center was his first target that offered him the live victims he wanted.

Witnesses reported the shooting to police, who began pursuing Muhammad as he left the scene. He accidentally drove into a construction zone, where he was forced to stop and was arrested without incident.

He was wearing an ammunition belt as he climbed out of his black pickup truck. He reportedly told police, "It's a war going on against Muslims and that's why I did it."

Weapons and equipment found in his truck included the SKS rifle, a Mossberg International 702 rifle with scope and laser sight, a Lorcin L-380 semi-automatic handgun, a .22-caliber pistol, 562 rounds of ammunition, sound suppressors, binoculars and two military books. In his apartment, police found Molotov cocktails.

Arkansas prosecutors charged Muhammad with capital murder, attempted capital murder and 10 counts of unlawful discharge of a weapon. The prosecutors announced they would seek the death penalty.

While evidence still was being gathered for the trial, Muhammad wrote a letter to the judge saying he wanted to plead guilty. He described himself as a "soldier in al Qaeda in the Arabian Peninsula." He also said he made his decision to plead guilty of his own free will, not the result of insanity. His attorneys later convinced Muhammad to change his plea to not guilty.

His attorneys claimed Muhammad suffered "a delusional disorder." During the 2011 trial, Muhammad changed his plea to guilty once again, which was accepted by prosecutors and the judge. He was sentenced to life in prison.

Muhammad's father described his son's transformation to extremism during a 2011 Congressional hearing on domestic Muslim radicals. He said his son was "trained and programmed" to kill in Yemen.

"Our children are in danger," Melvin Bledsoe told lawmakers. "It seems to me that Americans are sitting around doing nothing about radical extremists. This is a big elephant in the room."

Nidal Malik Hasan proclaimed "Allahu Akbar," or "God is the Greatest," as he burst into the Fort Hood, Texas, Soldier Readiness Center with a handgun on Nov. 5, 2009.

Army Sergeant Alonzo Lunsford recalled during a preliminary court hearing a few weeks later being puzzled by Hasan's outburst as he walked into the room.

"After that, I looked at him and wondered why he would say Allahu Akbar," Lunsford testified.

Then Lunsford saw Hasan's handgun. "I noticed the weapon he was firing had an infrared beam," the Army sergeant said.

Lunsford closed his eyes as one of the bullets Hasan fired struck him in the head over his left eye.

During the 10 minutes of the worst one-man terrorist attack against a military base on U.S. soil, Hasan killed 13 people and injured 29 others.

Some soldiers crouched into defensive positions the way they were trained while others fled the building. A civilian policewoman named Kimberly Munley who pulled up to the scene saw Hasan chasing a wounded soldier. The two of them exchanged gunfire, wounding Munley in the thigh and knee.

A second police officer arrived and immediately shot at Hasan, knocking him to the ground and seriously injuring him. As Hasan lost consciousness, the officer kicked the gun out of his hand and handcuffed him.

Hasan, an Army major and military psychiatrist, was scheduled to be deployed to Afghanistan three weeks later. Just before the shooting, he told a local storekeeper that he was bothered about his upcoming deployment because he might be required to fight or kill his fellow Muslims.

Otherwise, no one noticed anything unusual about Hasan's behavior. He started giving away his furniture in anticipation of his deployment. A fellow Muslim and military officer who prayed with him on the day of the shooting said he appeared relaxed and gave no obvious signs of any threat.

Hasan was investigated previously by the FBI and military intelligence but was cleared of suspicion. He came to their attention when military intelligence intercepted 18 emails he exchanged with Anwar al-Awlaki, the American-born Muslim cleric and chief propagandist for al Qaeda. Al-Awlaki wrote in a February 2009 blog entry, "I pray that Allah destroys America and all its allies."

In one email, Hasan wrote to al-Awlaki to say, "I can't wait to join you" in heaven. He also asked al-Awlaki whether Islam would allow innocent persons to be killed in a suicide attack and when jihad is appropriate.

A fellow Fort Hood Muslim later said Hasan's eyes "lit up" when he discussed al-Awlaki. Investigators believe his conversations with al-Awlaki pushed him over the brink into violence while he dealt with depression.

Al-Awlaki denied directly influencing Hasan to shoot anyone in a media interview after the Foot Hood violence. He reportedly told Yemeni journalist Abdulelah Hider Shaea, "Maybe Nidal was affected by one of my lectures." He added, "It was clear from his emails that Nidal trusted me. Nidal told me, 'I speak with you about issues that I never speak with anyone else.'"

The Joint Terrorism Task Force led by the FBI reviewed the emails along with Army analysts. The Army personnel concluded Hasan must have been doing research on behalf of the more than 10,000 Muslims in the U.S. armed forces.

On another occasion, Hasan posted a message on the social website Scribd that said, "If one suicide bomber can kill 100 enemy soldiers because they were caught off guard, that would be considered a strategic victory." The FBI did not investigate the posting thoroughly because of uncertainties about whether Hasan wrote it and whether the writer was advocating a terrorist attack.

After the Fort Hood shootings, the FBI came under criticism for overlooking the implied threat in Hasan's Internet postings and emails he exchanged with al-Awlaki.

"Emailing a known al Qaeda sympathizer should have set off alarm bells," former CIA officer and Middle Eastern expert Bruce Riedel told the Dallas Morning News. "Even if he was exchanging recipes, the bureau should have put out an alert."

Charles Allen, the Homeland Security Department's former chief intelligence officer, said, "I find it difficult to understand why an Army major would be in repeated contact with an Islamic extremist like Anwar al-Awlaki, who preaches a hateful ideology directed at inciting violence against the United States and the West. It is hard to see how repeated contact would in any legitimate way further his research as a psychiatrist."

Comments from radical Muslims showed a far different sentiment about the Fort Hood shootings.

Al Qaeda spokesman Adam Gadahn called Hasan a "Mujahid brother" who "has shown us what one righteous Muslim with an assault rifle can do for his religion and brothers in faith." He described Hasan as "a pioneer, a trailblazer and a role model."

Like many of the lone wolves who strike out with violence, little in Hasan's background aroused suspicions.

He was born in the Washington, D.C., suburbs of Arlington County, Virginia to Palestinian parents. He grew up helping his parents run their restaurant in Roanoke and graduated from high school in 1988.

He joined the Army immediately after high school and served as an enlisted soldier while attending Virginia Tech University. He graduated in 1997 with a bachelor's degree in biochemistry. He then attended medical school at Uniformed Services University of the Health Sciences and did his residency in psychiatry at Walter Reed Army Medical Center.

At Walter Reed, he made a presentation to staff members entitled, "The Quranic World View as It Relates to Muslims in the U.S. Military." Some attendees criticized Hasan's presentation, particularly his suggestion that the Defense Department "should allow Muslim soldiers the option of being released as 'conscientious objectors' to increase troop morale and decrease adverse events. The adverse events he described included killing of fellow soldiers.

Other signs of trouble arose after a lone wolf terrorist shot two Army recruiters at Little Rock, Ark., on June 1, 2009. Hasan's colleagues said he seemed disturbed by the incident and became more argumentative with them.

They also noticed that he was bothered by statements of soldiers returning from Afghanistan and Iraq who Hasan was treating for post-traumatic stress disorder. Some of the soldiers described what they did to Muslims during battle.

Hasan started telling his colleagues that Muslims should oppose the American military presence in Afghanistan and Iraq. He also said President Barack Obama should withdraw the troops.

His relatives described him as quiet, religious and someone who disliked violence but that he occasionally fell victim to harassment by his fellow soldiers because of his Muslim background.

His aunt, Noel Hasan of Falls Church, Va., told The Washington Post the harassment he endured after the Sept. 11, 2001 terrorist attacks prompted him to consider leaving the military.

"I know what that is like," Hasan's aunt reportedly said. "Some people can take it and some cannot. He had listened to all of that, and he wanted out of the military, and they would not let him leave even after he offered to repay [for his medical training]."

Other relatives described how sensitive he was as a child. He once fainted while watching a childbirth and another time grieving for months after a pet bird died.

His decision to join the U.S. military was influenced partly by family pride after his uncle and cousins served in the Army. He won the National Defense Service Medal twice, first during the Gulf War then during the war on terrorism in Iraq and Afghanistan. He also won the Global War on Terrorism Service Medal.

In other words, no one suspected anything seriously wrong about U.S. Army Major Nidal Malik Hasan until he showed up at Fort Hood's Soldier Readiness Center and randomly shot more than three dozen people.

Lone wolf terrorism is not unique to Muslims. In fact, the most deadly act of this type of terrorism in U.S. history was committed by Timothy McVeigh, who was known only as a loyal American from the Midwest heartland until he detonated a truck bomb in Oklahoma City on April 19, 1995. The explosion killed 168 people and injured more than 600.

He targeted a federal government office building in retaliation for a deadly police attack against a religious group in Waco, Texas a year earlier.

The difference is that radical Muslims represent a lone wolf threat that shows no sign of diminishing as their faith in Islam drives them to violence, particularly against the United States.

AL QAEDA TAKES THE LEAD

AL QAEDA, WHICH translates to The Base, was born in 1988 in the waning days of the Soviet war in Afghanistan. Muslim fighters training to fight the Soviets referred to their camp as "the base," which took root as the name for the entire militant Muslim movement.

As the Soviets withdrew, they left behind battle-hardened Muslim radicals who had traveled to Afghanistan in the 1980s to defend against what they believed was a war on Islam.

They came from all over the Arab world, were known informally as the "Arab Afghans" and agreed they did not want to leave their common bond of defending Islam. They were united in their belief a Christian-Jewish alliance conspired to destroy their religion.

Under the leadership of a wealthy cleric trained and funded by the U.S. military named Osama bin Laden, they decided to search for other jihads, or holy wars.

A primary goal of the group became to launch jihad against the United States and its allies in Christian countries to eliminate the world's man-made laws and replace them with the strict Islamic law called sharia.

After the Soviets pulled out of Afghanistan, their next opportunity arose in 1991 during the Gulf War, when Iraq invaded Kuwait to seize its oil fields and abundant revenue. If the war had remained a purely Arab dispute, al Qaeda might not have been able to unite militant Muslims.

But it was not only an Arab war. Instead, it drew in "infidels," or Westerners, from the United States and Europe to rid Kuwait of invaders and eliminate the Iraqi threat to the world's oil supply. Along the way, U.S. and allied troops took up positions in cities such as Mecca and Medina along with other Islamic holy sites.

Al Qaeda remained a ragtag, mostly forgotten group during the Gulf War. As Westerners pounded their Arab enemies into submission with bombs, tanks and machine guns, sympathy for splinter group radicals grew.

Al Qaeda set up its headquarters in Sudan about the time of the U.S.-led invasion of Iraq. In 1996, the group moved to Afghanistan, where it organized about a dozen training camps and forged a close alliance with the Taliban.

They asserted their influence through terrorist attacks, beginning with the Feb. 26, 1993 truck bombing in the underground parking lot of New York's World Trade Center. Around noon, Eyad Ismoil drove a rented truck packed with 1,336 pounds of urea nitrate-hydrogen gas explosives into the parking lot under the North Tower of the World Trade Center. He climbed out, lit the fuse and ran.

The al Qaeda planners hoped to tumble the North Tower into the South Tower, collapsing both of them and killing tens of thousands of people. Instead, the blast knocked a 98-foot hole into four sublevels of the North Tower but did not collapse the highly reinforced building.

Six people died and more than a thousand were injured, most during the unorganized rush to evacuate the building or from smoke inhalation. Six al Qaeda associates were convicted of charges that included conspiracy, interstate transportation of explosives and explosive destruction of property.

Rather than being considered villains, many Muslims considered them heroes who provided inspiration for their supporters.

The 1993 truck bombing was followed by other al Qaeda attacks. They included the June 1996 truck bomb that killed 19 U.S. soldiers and injured 498 people near Dhahran, Saudi Arabia. The bomb was hidden in a fuel truck and exploded outside a high-rise apartment building that housed the sleeping American soldiers.

On Aug. 7, 1998, simultaneous truck bombs at the U.S. embassies in Dar es Salaam, Tanzania, and Nairbobi, Kenya, killed hundreds of people. The bombings coincided with the eighth anniversary of the arrival of U.S. troops in Saudi Arabia. They also prompted the FBI to put Osama bin Laden on their 10 Most Wanted list.

Two years later, on Oct. 12, 2000, suicide bombers floated a small boat into the side of the USS Cole as it refueled at the port of Aden in Yemen. The more than 400 pounds of explosives it carried blew a 40-foot by 40-foot gash in the ship's galley, killing 17 American sailors and wounding 39 as they lined up for lunch.

The crew stopped the flooding and prevented the ship from sinking. Nonetheless, it was the most deadly attack on a U.S. Naval vessel since 1987.

Less than a year later, al Qaeda launched its signature terrorist attack by slamming airline jets into New York's World Trade Center, the Pentagon and the Pennsylvania countryside.

The September 11 attack created both a problem and an opportunity for al Qaeda. U.S. military strikes on its bases and training camps dispersed the group across the Arab world and decentralized its leadership.

However, the September 11 attacks also gave al Qaeda the credibility it needed to attract more sympathizers and fighters.

Since the attack, U.S. intelligence agencies report al Qaeda's influence appears to have grown to the point it operates in more than 40 countries, including in Europe and in North America. Suspected terrorist cells have been traced to New York, London, Madrid, Milan and Hamburg.

Even the stateless expanse of al Qaeda across the globe fits well with its strategy for jihad. Its leaders hope to stage attacks in so many diverse places and ways that the United States would get drawn into conflicts scattered around the world while suffering catastrophic economic damage from the aggression. Eventually, the U.S. economy and military could not support such a broad deployment, thereby giving al Qaeda an opportunity to operate without resistance.

However, the U.S. counter-strategy took a heavy toll on al Qaeda. Rather than striking hard with large bombs and armored divisions that would inflict massive death tolls, the U.S. military instead used narrowly targeted attacks to hit al Qaeda's leadership.

Airborne drone strikes, as well as assassinations and arrests based on intelligence reports, culminated in the death of Osama bin Laden at his home in Pakistan on May 2, 2011, at the hands of U.S. Navy Seals.

As their top-down leadership disintegrated, al Qaeda merely shifted gears to a fallback structure that is hard to monitor by intelligence agencies. The London-based pan-Arab newspaper A-Quds Al-Arabi (Arab Jerusalem) described al Qaeda's management style in a 2005 report as "centralization of decision and decentralization of execution."

Associated groups, or cells, were given broad discretion to stake out and hit targets, preferably in the United States. At the same time, the organization's propaganda officers, such as Anwar al-Awlaki and Adam Gadahn, encouraged lone wolf attacks through emails and Internet postings. Al-Awlaki's admirers included Tamerlan Tsarnaev.

A key to al Qaeda's longevity has been its elusiveness. The loosely connected networks come together for a specific act or project, then disappear into unassuming lives in the rest of their host countries' populations.

Their training camps come and go as well, often operating in Somalia, Yemen, Chechnya and the Afghanistan mountains. They can change form and location as the need arises but never completely disappear.

A 2014 U.S. Senate Select Committee on Intelligence report suggested al Qaeda might refer to a shared idea among various groups that include elements of the Taliban, the Egyptian group Islamic Jihad, radical Sunni Muslims, the mujahideen youth movement called al-Shabaab in Somalia and a variety of lone wolves.

Bin Laden hinted at his group's transient nature in an October 2001 media interview when he said, "... this matter isn't about any specific person... is not about the al Qaeda organization. We are the children of an Islamic Nation, with Prophet Muhammad as its leader, our Lord is one ... and all the true believers are brothers. So the situation isn't like the West portrays it, that there is an organization with a specific name and so on."

The core group that identifies itself as al Qaeda might be as small as a few hundred zealots, according to U.S. intelligence sources. But their interconnections with other groups give them a potential fighting force numbering in the thousands.

Much of the early information about its structure came from Jamal Ahmed Mohamed al-Fadl, a former bin Laden associate who was trained as a Sudanese militant. He fought in the Afghan war after being recruited through the Farouq mosque in Brooklyn, where he lived in the 1980s. He joined al Qaeda in 1988 and took a loyalty oath to bin Laden.

After bin Laden accused him of skimming $110,000 in al Qaeda money and demanded that he repay it, al-Fadl instead became an informant for U.S. intelligence agencies.

He told the FBI and others that al Qaeda's operations were divided among five main committees.

The Military Committee acquires weapons, plans attacks and trains commandoes. The Law Committee reviews al Qaeda's proposed actions to ensure they conform with the strict Islamic Sharia law. A Media Committee handled public relations and ran a newspaper until the late 1990s but it was replaced by a broadcast production enterprise in 2005 that compiled video and audio for al Qaeda.

The Islamic Study/Fatwah Committee issues religious edicts intended to guide the thoughts and actions of its followers.

Traditionally, fatwahs have been issued by Islamic scholars, such as Syria's Grand Mufti Ahmad Badruddin Hassoud, who prohibited any kind of smoking by Muslims. An April 14, 2004 fatwah from Yusuf al-Qaradawi said Muslims should boycott all products from Israel and the United States. Muslim Brotherhood leader Sheikh Sadeq Abdallah bin Al-Majed issued a fatwah forbidding vaccinations for children, claiming they are a conspiracy by Jews and Freemasons.

Osama bin Laden issued two fatwahs that came to define part of al Qaeda's ideology.

His 1996 fatwah was entitled "Declaration of War Against the Americans Occupying the Land of the Two Holy Places." It was faxed to his supporters around the world and published by the Arabic newspaper Al-Quds Al-Arabi, but gained little notoriety in 1996, before bin Laden became a household name.

It complained about the American influence in several countries, particularly Saudi Arabia.

His 1998 fatwah entitled "Declaration of the World Islamic Front for Jihad Against Jews and Crusaders" drew much more attention. Five other radical Muslim leaders joined bin Laden as signatories.

In addition to complaining about the U.S. military presence in the Middle East and American support for Israel, the fatwah claimed to establish the religious authorization for killing Americans and Jews anywhere in the world, even civilians.

"To kill Americans and their allies, both civil and military, is an individual duty of every Muslim who is able, in any country where this is possible, until the Aqsa Mosque [in Jerusalem] and the Haram Mosque [in Mecca] are freed from their grip and until their armies, shattered and broken-winged, depart from all the lands of Islam, incapable of threatening any Muslim," the fatwah said.

After citing authorities in the Koran, the document said, "By God's leave, we call on every Muslim who believes in God and hopes for reward to obey God's command to kill the Americans and plunder their possessions wherever he finds them and whenever he can. Likewise we call on the Muslim ulema and leaders and youth and soldiers to launch attacks against the armies of the American devils and against those who are allied with them from among the helpers of Satan."

The innovation that has kept al Qaeda agile and difficult to quash is the Money/Business Committee. It uses the hawala banking system in which debts and payments are conducted through an honor system of participating brokers.

Typically, a customer gives a broker in one city an amount of money the customer wants transferred to someone else in another city. The customer also tells the broker a password the money recipient is supposed to repeat.

The first broker then contacts a second broker in the place where the money is going and tells him the password. The person receiving the money approaches the second broker and tells him the password. The second broker then pays the money, minus a small commission.

The second broker can then collect payment from the first broker. The payment could be money, property, labor or anything else the two brokers agree will settle the debt.

As many as 1,000 of the unregulated banks, or hawaladers,

may be operating in Pakistan alone, according to U.S. intelligence sources. They have handled deals for as much as $10 million.

Al Qaeda operates on a budget of about $30 million a year, the U.S. Congress' 9/11 Commission report said. The money from hawala transactions have funded airplane tickets for al Qaeda agents, paid their salaries, funded businesses and been used to purchase fake passports.

Police in Western countries have arrested suspected al Qaeda agents, frozen their assets and shut down companies acting as fronts for their operations. Interrogations of al Qaeda members incarcerated at Guantanamo Bay, Cuba, helped gather intelligence for police raids.

Getting rid of the entire organization is a far different task. Despite setbacks that included the deaths or arrests of its top leaders, al Qaeda "remains vibrant and effective," according to a 2004 report from the Oxford Research Group.

ISIS SEES AN OPPORTUNITY

THE HAMMERING AL Qaeda endured from the U.S. military drummed up sympathy and support among other radical Muslims.

For years, they were divided among various Muslim Sunni groups. On April 9, 2013, they united as a single organization using the name Islamic State of Iraq and the Levant (ISIL), also Islamic State of Iraq and Syria (ISIS). The Levant refers to a region of the Middle East that includes Jordan, Israel, Gaza, Lebanon and Cyprus.

As they burst into the headlines in 2014 with military strikes, mass murders and a videotaped beheading of American journalist James Foley, even the most jaded political and military leaders were appalled.

"They're beyond any terrorist group," Defense Secretary Chuck Hagel said during a Pentagon press briefing. "They marry ideology, sophistication of strategic and tactical military prowess. They are tremendously well-funded. Oh, this is beyond anything that we've seen, so we must prepare for everything, and the only way you do that is you take a cold, steely hard look at it and get ready."

The main thing that distinguished ISIS from al Qaeda was their extreme radical ideology.

They used military tactics intended to bring all the world's Muslims together into a single empire ruled by a caliph, or religious leader. After initially showing support for al Qaeda, the two groups split over disagreements about the degree of violence that should be used to achieve their goals.

Al Qaeda leaders announced the split in February 2014, calling ISIS too brutal and complaining about the group's "notorious intractability."

The United Nations Security Council — joined by the United States, Australia, Canada, Indonesia, Saudi Arabia and the United Kingdom — have officially declared ISIS to be a terrorist organization.

Even among Islamic nations, militant Sunnis like those found in ISIS create controversy. The suspicion that commonly falls on them for their strict interpretation and adherence to sharia law has made them outcasts. The discrimination they often encounter also has drawn them closer together for mutual support and made them even more radical.

Much of their reprisal is directed at moderate Shia Muslims and — more than anyone — Christians.

ISIS claimed about 15,000 warriors by the summer of 2014 but also claimed their numbers were growing along with their military expansion in Iraq. Along the way, they have killed thousands of civilians, often with U.S.-made weapons stolen from the Iraqi government.

On June 29, 2014, as the rest of the world bemoaned their brutality, ISIS renamed itself "Islamic State" to reflect its intention to unite Muslims worldwide, instead of only in the Middle East. The group also named Abu Bakr al-Baghdadi, now called Amir al-Mu'minim Caliph Ibrahim, as its leader.

Like al Qaeda, ISIS's ideology is an outgrowth of the Muslim Brotherhood that was organized in the 1920s as the world's first modern Islamic group.

The Muslim Brotherhood was considered extremist when it started, but nothing like ISIS. ISIS interprets Islam to justify staunch anti-Western policies, violence in the name of religion and targeting anyone who disagrees with them as infidels.

The best way to purify present-day Islam from corrupt influence is through jihad, or holy war, according to ISIS. Their top targets are Israel and the Western countries they believe are creating the corruption.

As a first step toward broader conflict, ISIS has been fighting with the Palestinian Sunni group Hamas. ISIS leaders consider Hamas too weak-willed in its struggles against Israel.

By removing Hamas, ISIS leaders believe they will clear their way to gain a greater leadership role for Sunnis and for direct conflict with Israel and its allies.

By mid-2014, ISIS had experienced limited success in establishing its control over parts of Syria and Iraq. The group also released a video in which an English-speaking announcer described ISIS's plans to eliminate all modern borders between Muslim countries in the Middle East.

Increasingly, its fighters came from places far from either Iraq or Syria. The Economist magazine reported that by the summer of 2014, ISIS had drawn about 3,000 fighters from foreign countries. Many came from Chechnya but about 500 came from France, Britain and other European countries.

The U.S. government tracked as many as 300 Americans who joined ISIS and represented a significant threat to the United States. The concerns were fed partly by reports that a California man was the first American to die while fighting for ISIS in Syria. The body of Douglas McAuthur McCain, 33, was found with an American passport in his pocket after a fierce battle.

About the same time, ISIS published photographs on the social network site Twitter designed to foment fear among Americans. One of them showed an ISIS black flag in front of the

White House. A second one taken in front of a Chicago skyscraper carried the message, "We are in your state. We are in your cities. We are in your streets. You are our goals everywhere."

U.S. military analysts say ISIS operates with a strong top-down management style that regularly measures the success or failure of its armed tactics, which is a clear indication the group conducts itself as an army.

Much of their expertise was honed during the Syrian civil war that started in the spring of 2011 with nationwide protests against President Bashar al-Assad's government. Assad responded with a military crackdown.

Popular outrage against the crackdown grew to a civil war that included rebel groups like ISIS. By late 2014, ISIS controlled a third of Syria and most of its gas and oil production.

Former U.S. Secretary of State Hillary Clinton blamed the fractionalized, leaderless nature of the uprising against Assad for the rise of terrorist groups like ISIS.

"The failure to help build up a credible fighting force of the people who were the originators of the protests against Assad — there were Islamists, there were secularist, there was everything in the middle — the failure to do that left a big vacuum, which the jihadists have now filled."

As ISIS grows, it increasingly operates like a government. It provides social services to fellow Sunnis and religious lectures and evangelism to potential converts. Its most controversial services include courts, which can lead to death sentences for the group's opponents.

One of its most successful ventures is its propaganda efforts. ISIS operates at least three media divisions to produce web-based propaganda, videos, posters and pamphlets. Some of it is translated into English, French, German and Russian to help its foreign recruiting.

Its social media campaign is primarily focused on Twitter, which ISIS uses to send Tweets to supporters and anyone else that uses popular hashtags.

Its finances are derived from tactics similar to its military incursions.

Iraqi intelligence services reported in mid-2014 that a captured ISIS leader said under questioning the group held assets of about $2 billion.

Part of its funding is believed to come from smuggling weapons and drugs. Another portion is believed to come from ransom money they get from kidnappings. Extortion money from truck drivers seeking safe passage or business owners threatened with bombings provides another part of the funds.

When ISIS overran the Iraqi city of Mosul in 2014, the group is believed to have stolen as much as $429 million from the city's central bank. Additional sums are believed to have come from stealing gold bullion from several banks.

Other parts of the organization are run like a legitimate business, such as a division that produces crude oil from oilfields it controls in Eastern Syria and another one that sells electricity to the Syrian government that it generates by hydroelectric dams.

Since 2012, ISIS has produced annual reports listing its funding sources in an apparent effort to attract donors.

Only about 5% of its funds came from donations in the first few years it operated. The controversy centers on the identity of the donors. Iranian and Iraqi leaders have accused the governments of Saudi Arabia and Qatar of donating funds to ISIS, but so far the claims are unproven.

Another part of the controversy focuses on what ISIS does with the money. It is known ISIS leaders redistribute much of the money to militant cells operating in various cities.

Intelligence communities would like to know the locations of the cells and the cities where they operate, particularly if any of them are located in Western countries.

ISIS militants are just "one plane ticket away from U.S. shores," Rep. Mike Rogers (R-Mich.) said during an Aug. 24,

2014 appearance on NBC News' "Meet the Press." Rogers was chairman of the House Intelligence Committee.

"One of the problems is it's gone unabated for nearly two years, and that draws people from Britain to across Europe, and even the United States, to go and join the fight," Rogers said. "They see that as a winning ideology, a winning strategy and they want to be part of it. And that's what makes it so dangerous."

Most of the military equipment ISIS uses — nearly all of it stolen in Iraq and Syria — would be useless to terrorist cells or lone wolves. It includes T-72 main battle tanks, M198 howiters, AT-4 anti-tank weapons, Stinger surface-to-air missiles, Humvees, BM-21 Grad multiple rocket launchers and at least one Scud missile.

ISIS seized American-made UH-60 Blackhawk helicopters and cargo planes when it seized Mosul Airport in June 2014 but so far is not known to have used them.

The less bulky equipment ISIS acquired might be out of sight but not out of mind for the international intelligence community. Iraq's United Nations ambassador has warned that nuclear material ISIS seized at Mosul University could be used to make a nuclear weapon. However, the International Atomic Energy Agency reports the material is too low grade to represent a serious terrorist threat.

No one doubts ISIS would use the weapons on Americans and their allies if they were given an opportunity. Since widespread political kidnappings started in Iraq in 2004, more than 200 of them were foreigners.

Americans were the prime targets of kidnappers, British second. ISIS is known to have participated in some of the kidnappings and subsequent murders, although the connection is unclear.

As of February 2015, at least 12 of the kidnapped murder victims were American. Another 12 either escaped, were released or left only suspicions about what happened to them.

Nicholas Evan Berg, a telecommunications contractor from Virginia, was one of the most famous American victims. He was beheaded on May 11, 2004 by Abu Musab al-Zarqawi, an ISIS founder. The beheading was videotaped and posted on the Internet, where it sparked widespread outrage before U.S. intelligence agencies took it down.

Al-Zarqawi also beheaded Owen Eugene "Jack" Armstrong, an American contractor working for the construction company Gulf Supplies Commercial Services. He was kidnapped Sept. 16, 2004 and killed four days later.

The next day, al-Zarqawi's group beheaded fellow American Kenneth Bigley.

By the time ISIS beheaded American journalist James Foley on Aug. 19, 2014, and threatened to kill another kidnapped American journalist, President Obama decided something more needed to be done.

He called ISIS a "cancer" that threatened Iraq and the entire region. He pledged to continue attacking the group even as its leaders ramped up their threats against Americans.

"We will be vigilant and we will be relentless," Obama said as the U.S. military planned more airstrikes against ISIS.

Similar fighting words mixed with caution went out in other countries.

In the United Kingdom, Prime Minister David Cameron announced his country would revoke the passports of citizens traveling to Syria.

The passport revocations were another British security measure after the government raised its terror threat level to "severe." He predicted the struggle against Islamic terrorists would be long and arduous.

"We are in the middle of a generational struggle against a poisonous and extremist ideology," Cameron said.

Britain's "severe" threat level is only one step below the highest, or "critical," level. Cameron said intelligence sources report a terrorist attack is likely.

"What we're facing in Iraq and Syria now with ISIL is a deeper and greater threat to our security than we have ever known before," the British prime minister said.

In a show of defiance, ISIS responded to the threats from Western leaders Sept. 2, 2014, by publishing on the Internet the beheading of Time magazine correspondent Steven Sotloff.

The masked militant who killed him said in the video that as long as U.S. airstrikes against ISIS continue, "our knife will continue to strike the necks of your people." The prime ISIS executioner spoke with a British accent and became known as "Jihadi John."

The FBI put out an advisory to local law enforcement agencies warning them of lone wolf attacks. The bulletin said the FBI was "unaware of any specific, credible threats against the homeland."

Nevertheless, the FBI warned it could not rule out attacks against the United States by sympathizers inspired by ISIS propaganda. Until the summer of 2014, most ISIS propaganda urged foreign fighters to join the fight in Syria and Iraq. As their influence grew, the group's recruiting effort broadened to ask for help anywhere they could get it.

ISIS extremists "have employed — and will almost certainly continue — Twitter 'hashtag' campaigns that have ... been able to quickly reach a global audience of potential violent extremists," the FBI said.

Examples of the propaganda put out by ISIS included the videotaped beheading of James Foley that was published on YouTube and a photo of the ISIS flag in front of the White House.

Another propaganda effort consisted of a video with a voiceover saying, "God willing, we will raise the flag of Allah in the White House."

In addition, the group was likely to use reports of American airstrikes to create a perception of a war with Islam that might incite Muslims to violence against the United States, the FBI said in its joint bulletin with the U.S. Homeland Security Department.

"We urge state and local authorities to promptly report suspicious activities related to homeland plotting and individuals interested in traveling to overseas conflict zones, such as Syria or Iraq, to fight with foreign terrorist organizations," the bulletin said.

"Because of the individualized nature of the radicalization process — it is difficult to predict triggers that will contribute to [homegrown radicals] attempting acts of violence," the FBI bulletin said. The lone wolf attackers "present law enforcement with limited opportunities to detect and disrupt plots, which frequently involve simple plotting against targets of opportunity."

Some experts cast doubt on the effectiveness of the FBI's efforts to stop lone wolf terrorism.

"A lone wolf terrorist is able to evade a lot of this surveillance because they blend in," John Rossomando, senior analyst with the Investigative Project on Terrorism, a Washington, D.C.-based advocacy organization, said in an interview. "They look like us, they act like us."

The Boston Marathon bombing suspects were a good example, he said. The accused bombers were members of the community who no one suspected of being anything more than a college student and an amateur boxer.

The Marathon bombing "fit with the pattern of bombings" encouraged by terrorist leaders. "They were definitely inspired by what they saw on the Internet," Rossomando said.

Among the lessons they learned was that the ease of concealing homemade low-tech weapons makes them the most threatening. Other examples include the Fort Hood shootings carried out by one man with a handgun and the Oklahoma City bomb that was made from bags of fertilizer.

"It would be just as easy to leave a bomb in a bag in Washington as in Boston," Rossomando said.

He said he believed Dzhokhar Tsarnaev was an accomplice in the Boston bombings but that even the death penalty would create no deterrence against other lone wolf terrorists.

"These people want to die," Rossomando said. "They want to be a martyr to their cause. I don't see it deterring anyone else who wants to try."

JURY SELECTION BEGINS

ONLY SIX DAYS before jury selection began on Jan. 5, 2015, Dzhokhar's attorneys still were asking for a change of venue.

Their pleas had taken them to the First Circuit Court of Appeals, where the panel of federal judges ruled 2-to-1 against a change of venue.

The defense team relied on the 10th Circuit's 1998 decision in United States v. Timothy McVeigh, which granted a change of venue in the Oklahoma City bomber's case because the "emotional burden of the explosion and its consequences" created "so great a prejudice" that the defendant "cannot obtain a fair and impartial trial" in the community where the attack occurred.

In McVeigh's case, the trial was transferred to Denver, where he was convicted and given the death penalty.

In Dzhokhar's case, the appeals court agreed with Judge O'Toole that the defense attorneys failed to meet their heavy burden of proving an impartial jury could not be found in Boston.

The lone dissenter was Judge Juan R. Torruella, who wrote, "Tsarnaev's argument that the entire city of Boston and its surrounding area was victimized — as evidenced by the city's virtual lockdown and the images of SWAT team members roaming the streets and knocking door-to-door in Watertown — is compelling."

Although O'Toole disagreed an impartial jury was impossible, he agreed it would be difficult. As a result, he decided to allow the jurors to be drawn from an unusually large pool of local residents.

On the first day of jury selection, 400 potential jurors lined up alphabetically the length of the federal courthouse. They were the first group among 1,373 Boston area residents who would form the pool of potential jurors. It was the largest selection of potential jurors in the history of Boston's John Joseph Moakley U.S. Courthouse.

Dzhokhar was escorted into the courtroom surrounded by U.S. marshals. Meanwhile, white Homeland Security vehicles were lined up bumper-to-bumper in front of the courthouse. Others circled the block looking for anything suspicious.

A dark special operations van was parked near the entrance. Boston police officers walked around the building on patrol while other officers roamed the hallways with bomb-sniffing dogs.

In the nearby harbor, armed U.S. Coast Guard boats ran up and down the waters within view of the courthouse. Media reports speculated that police snipers were hiding on nearby buildings.

Dzhokhar wore a collared sweater in the morning and crewneck in the afternoon on the first day of jury selection. Each of the potential jurors sat only a few feet from him as the judge spoke with them.

Some looked at him with curiosity while others seemed emotionless. They did not speak with one another. Dzhokhar watched some of the jurors during the morning session but paid closer attention to the judge in the afternoon.

The now 21-year-old fidgeted occasionally. He appeared slim and with flowing, curly hair and a beard. His defense team of five attorneys sat beside him.

After the first potential jurors took seats in the courtroom, O'Toole spoke with them to say this case "differs from other criminal cases in a significant way." The jurors might need to decide whether the defendant should die.

They don't need special experience or education, but "What you do need is a commitment to justice," O'Toole said.

Despite 1,373 people who could be interviewed, O'Toole said he would have 12 jurors and six alternates selected by Jan. 26 so the trial could begin "in proper." Instead, a slower-than-anticipated pace for questioning the potential jurors, along with delays from heavy snowfall, kept pushing the start date back.

Another difference compared with most criminal trials was the media attention. Television news trucks crowded the parking spaces, forcing one food truck driver to tweet that he could not come to his usual spot Jan. 5. The area already was taken by media trucks.

Also absent were the demonstrators who had showed up near the courthouse at previous hearings to loudly voice support for Tsarnaev. The judge ordered that they be kept away from the courthouse to avoid the risk of influencing jurors.

The selection process required that jurors be brought in to the courthouse in groups of 200 to fill out a questionnaire. Each questionnaire took about an hour.

The questions sought to identify persons who might be biased in favor of the law enforcement witnesses, others who identified strongly with the bombing victims and others who would be unwilling to impose a death sentence if Dzhokhar was convicted.

Legal experts described the process chosen by O'Toole as cautious, obviously intended to avoid errors in a high profile case.

Before the potential jurors filled out the questionnaires, O'Toole advised them to be complete and honest. He warned them to avoid media reports to maintain their impartiality.

"You must be able to decide the issues of the case, based on the evidence that is presented during the course of the trial, and not from any other source," O'Toole said. "We need your help and we need your honest performance in this important duty of citizenship."

Other than conversation with his attorneys, Dzhokhar spoke in open court only to answer four questions from the judge about his defense attorneys. O'Toole asked him whether he was satisfied with his defense team. Each time he responded, "Yes, sir."

Noticeably absent in his speech was the Russian accent he displayed when he pleaded not guilty during arraignment. His friends and neighbors said he normally did not have a Russian accent, meaning he appeared to use it consciously during the arraignment for reasons never explained.

As each set of potential jurors was brought into the courtroom, Dzhokhar nodded awkwardly to some but looked toward the floor other times. While O'Toole instructed them about the questionnaire, Dzhokhar sometimes picked at his beard, drummed his fingers on the table or watched the judge.

By the third day, he seemed to calm down slightly.

Only a few bombing victims sat in court to watch the jury selection. One of them was Jaymi Cohen, a Tufts University lacrosse player who was hit while watching the race from the sidelines with teammates. U.S. Attorney Carmen Ortiz sat beside Cohen and her father.

Tsarnaev's family members, who showed up to support him in previous hearings, did not appear for jury selection. Two of his uncles who live in Maryland angrily told reporters they either had to work or would not attend unless asked.

It was hard to determine from Dzhokhar's behavior whether he knew the importance of the jury selection for his trial.

Legal experts interviewed on Boston television stations said the evidence strongly indicated Dzhokhar would be found guilty.

The greatest unknown was whether the jury would sentence him to death.

Carol Rose, executive director of the American Civil Liberties Union of Massachusetts, wrote, "This trial won't really be about Tsarnaev's guilt or innocence. The evidence against him is overwhelming. The trial will be about us — about the kind of society in which we want to live and whether we will be ruled by our fears or by our values."

Legal commentators speculated that his attorneys would seek jurors who were willing to look beyond the facts of the bombings to consider why he might have participated in the plot. They would include people who are well-educated, enjoy traveling, interested in other cultures and religions and have a natural curiosity.

Prosecutors sought more conservative jurors known for regular work habits and comfortable lives who show a strong preference for law and order.

The contest between the defense and prosecution to choose the most favorable jurors weighed in favor of the government before jury selection started. Jurors had to be "death-qualified" before they could even be considered. In other words, they had to be willing to impose the death penalty or they would be disqualified.

The "death-qualified" criteria prompted some lawyers to say again that Massachusetts might not be the best place for the trial. The state's abolition of the death penalty in 1984 and continuing opposition to it in popular opinion polls meant only the most right-wing residents of Eastern Massachusetts were likely to be chosen as jurors.

A 2005 Death Penalty Information Center Report summed up the kinds of people who would be excluded from a death penalty trial. The list included, "Catholics who have heeded their church's call to end the death penalty, believers of all stripes who find the death penalty immoral, conservatives who hold that the government should not be trusted with so much power, and liberals who will not apply capital punishment because it is not meted out fairly — all will be eliminated if they adhere to these views. They will not be able to serve even in the guilt-innocence phase of the trial, where one's view on the death penalty should be irrelevant."

Before the first week of jury selection ended, another fact was emerging from the proceedings. The chances of a plea bargain were slipping away.

A defendant can plead guilty during any stage of a criminal case. The defense attorney submits the defendant's offer of a guilty plea and the Justice Department official overseeing the case decides whether to accept it. In Dzhokhar's case, the proper Justice Department official would be Attorney General Eric Holder. Both parties then present the deal to the judge for a final ruling.

But as a case moves closer to a verdict, the chances of a plea bargain become more remote.

"As a practical matter, the chances of a plea deal once a trial begins diminishes," Donald Stern, former U.S. Attorney for Massachusetts, told Boston television station WBUR. "There would have to be some showing that the case is weaker or the knowledge about the defendant is different from what was known a year ago when the case was filed for the attorney general, in all likelihood, to change his mind."

The likelihood of a change of heart by the government seemed distant when shortly before jury selection started, U.S. Attorney Carmen Ortiz issued a statement saying, "Nothing has changed since the Attorney General first authorized federal prosecutors to seek the death penalty in this case and the government will continue to move forward with the trial."

Even Dzhokhar's father, Anzor, seemed to have accepted what appeared to be inevitable when he told ABC News as jury selection started, "The Americans are going to harm my second son the same way they did to my oldest son. We already know what's going to happen. Everything is in Allah's hand."

While jury selection continued, a Jan. 7, 2015 terrorist incident in Paris heightened the public outcry against Islamic extremists.

Three men associated with al Qaeda raided the offices of satirical magazine Charlie Hebdo, killing 12 people. The magazine had published cartoons mocking Islamist prophet Mohammed.

The last of the 12 people executed was a police officer who lay on the ground after being injured by gunfire. His last words appeared to be "No more, no more," before one of the terrorists fired point blank into his head with an automatic rifle. All of it was taped on video from the mobile telephones of witnesses.

The outcry against the terrorist strike spread across the Atlantic Ocean.

"Against the backdrop of jury selection for Dzhokhar Tsarnaev, it's like Boston is reliving what happened all over again," Rep. William Keating (D-Mass.) said. "I'm watching what's happening in Paris and I'm thinking of Watertown."

Dzhokhar's lawyers responded by filing a request with the judge to suspend jury selection for at least a month to let emotions from the Paris attack simmer down.

The Paris attack put the Boston Marathon bombings "at the center of a grim global drama," the attorneys wrote. A delay would allow time "for the extraordinary prejudice flowing from these events — and the comparison to those events to those at issue in this case — to diminish."

With the unruffled efficiency that had become his trademark during 20 years on the bench, Judge O'Toole denied their request.

"My detailed review of juror questionnaires in preparation for voir dire has so far confirmed, rather than undermined, my judgment that a fair and impartial jury can and will be chosen to determine the issues in this case," O'Toole wrote in an order.

The same kind of matter-of-fact style ran through his other statements from the bench and written rulings, some of which took up only a few pages on complex legal issues. Attorneys who know O'Toole describe him as the kind of judge that politicians who appointed him would want as a judge.

On the first day of jury selection, as the media, protesters, police and curiosity-seekers clamored in an out of the courtroom, O'Toole said with characteristic aplomb, "I think this will be brief."

O'Toole, who was 67 years old when the Tsarnaev trial started, graduated from Boston College in 1969 and Harvard Law School in 1972. From there, his career followed the straight arrow path typical of federal judges.

He was a partner at the large law firm of Hale & Dorr when he was appointed as a judge to the Boston Municipal Court in 1982. Governor Michael Dukakis appointed him to the Superior Court in 1990.

President Bill Clinton nominated him to a federal judgeship in 1995. The Senate easily confirmed him.

His reputation as a federal judge grew out of complex civil and criminal cases he oversaw. One of them was the lawsuit by famed crime writer Patricia Cornwell, who won a $51 million jury verdict against her former financial advisor. O'Toole later ordered a new trial after finding an error in one of his own rulings.

When he presided over the terrorism trial of Tarek Mehanna, who was convicted of supporting al Qaeda, the defendant launched into a harsh criticism of U.S. foreign policy and the prosecutor. O'Toole's dispassionate response consisted of sentencing Mehanna to 17-and-a-half years in prison.

In his private life, O'Toole is known for liking football, opera, history, playing the trumpet and occasional basketball games with colleagues.

On Jan. 15, 2015, jury selection moved to the second phase

with direct questioning of the potential jurors. The attorney and the judge had read through the 28-page juror questionnaires to weed out anyone with a conflict.

After the first 20 of the second phase potential jurors were brought into the courtroom, O'Toole gave them instructions in a somber tone that included telling them they might need to impose the death penalty.

"The jury, and not the judge, is responsible for determining whether a defendant convicted of a capital crime will live or die," O'Toole said.

O'Toole did most of the talking during the questioning, asking them about their backgrounds, their personal opinions of Dzhokhar and what they think of the death penalty. The attorneys occasionally asked follow-up questions.

One of the first prospective jurors interviewed was an advertising account manager.

"I would sentence him to death," he said as Dzhokhar stared at him while clutching a pen and sitting next to the defense attorneys. "I can't imagine any evidence that would change how I feel about what happened or what I think happened."

Another prospective juror, a project manager for insurance company John Hancock, said his wife was an intensive care nurse who treated marathon bombing victims.

"It's tough because it hit my wife hard — the stuff she had to do with the patients," he said.

He said he could sentence Dzhokhar to death but only if the evidence of guilt was strong. "To put someone to death it has to be 100 percent, rock solid, no doubt," he said.

A Catholic theologian interviewed as a prospective juror said the death penalty was out of the question for him.

"There's no way in modern America today ... that I am going to vote for the death penalty. I will not," he said.

Other potential jurors discussed whether the intense media coverage would influence their opinions.

"I don't know this guy over here from Adam," said a software programmer.

The evidence at trial would form the basis of his jury vote, he said. "I don't get swayed by the media," he said. "I don't get swayed by anybody."

For about half the prospective jurors, it was obvious to everyone they never could be considered impartial. Many came with vignettes about people they knew who were injured in the bombings or narrowly escaped being hit by shrapnel.

One woman said she lived in the same neighborhood as 8-year-old Martin Richard, who was killed while standing alongside his family. She said she met the boy during a neighborhood cleanup.

"I was just walking by a memorial for him," she said as her voice shook with emotion.

During much of the questioning, Dzhokhar avoided eye contact with the prospective jurors. Occasionally he would write on a legal pad in front of him on the defense table. His hair was neatly cut compared with the scruffy, curly style of his hair during earlier hearings.

Dzhokhar's attorneys made it clear early in the jury selection that they did not like O'Toole's line of questioning. Many of his questions focused on the death penalty instead of possible juror bias in deciding guilt or innocence.

"Our question is not about penalty, it's about guilt," defense attorney David Bruck told the judge. "I think that's where the rubber hits the road."

He added, "Can these jurors really presume this man innocent? Or is it, 'We all know he's guilty so let's get on to the penalty phase?' We're supposed to have a fair trial and the trial isn't supposed to be over already."

In response, O'Toole modified his questions to ask the potential jurors whether they would demand prosecutors prove Dzhokhar's guilt beyond a reasonable doubt before they would convict him. He also asked whether they had preexisting ideas about the defendant's guilt that would force the defense to prove his innocence.

The modified line of questioning did not convince the defense team that they could find an impartial jury in the wounded city of Boston.

They filed a third motion to get the trial moved to another city. "Fully 68 percent of the prospective jurors already believe that Mr. Tsarnaev is guilty before hearing a single witness or examining a shred of evidence at trial," they wrote in their change of venue motion.

The defense attorneys quoted excerpts from juror questionnaires in their motion.

"Why waste time on this guy you know he is guilty," one answer to the questionnaire said. Another prospective juror wrote, "We all know he's guilty so quit wasting everybody's time with a jury and string him up." Another one wrote, "For this case I think a public execution would be appropriate, preferable by bomb at the finish line of the marathon."

The defense motion said, "If this case does not warrant a change of venue, the entire body of law on venue as it relates to the constitutional rights to due process and a fair trial will be left a hollow shell."

Once again, O'Toole rejected the motion. The third request for a change of venue "has even less, not more, merit than the prior ones," the judge wrote in written order.

He wrote, "Contrary to the defendant's assertions, the voir dire process is successfully identifying potential jurors who are capable of serving as fair and impartial jurors in this case."

He also rejected a motion from the Boston Globe, which asked that court deliberations to decide which jurors are selected and which are sent home be open to the public. The questioning of potential jurors was public but the deliberations on who to choose were done privately between the attorneys and the judge.

The Globe's motion cited the "First Amendment rights of the public" to know about the trial process. O'Toole said the more important issue was to protect the jury process. Some potential jurors could stage their answers to questions if they knew in advance what they needed to say to be chosen, the judge said.

As the drama unfolded in the Moakley Courthouse, another show was being put on outside the court. Dzhokhar had attracted his own fan club.

Initially, they consisted mostly of teenaged girls who believed he was both innocent and handsome. Shortly after his arrest, they exchanged speculations by text message at *#FreeJahar hashtag* about his innocence and commented on his good looks.

Some of them showed up at his first hearings holding signs that demanded he be freed. By the time jury selection started, the teeny-boppers were mostly gone, replaced by a handful of die-hard women in their 30s and 40s who were concerned about what they claim was the injustice of prosecuting Dzhokhar.

They would hold up signs outside the courthouse proclaiming his innocence, discuss the case in online forums and organize protests. Some of them faced off with angry bombing victims.

One of their signs read, "FBI Entrapment = False Conviction." Another one said, "Exonerate Jahar."

Perhaps the most visible and vocal among his supporters was Karin Friedemann, a Boston freelance writer. She told the news web site Masslive.com that Dzhokhar was being framed by the government. Like his other supporters, she said Dzhokhar was too young and vulnerable to be blamed for the marathon bombing.

"He's almost like a Christ figure," Friedemann told Masslive.com.

She also reportedly said, "He's someone that you can easily relate to. When you see other psycho killers on the TV, they look like psycho killers, but Jahar doesn't look like that."

After one session of Dzhokhar's pre-trial hearing that Friedemann attended, she wrote in her blog, "He looked thin and seemed physically weak ... Jahar sported wild, unkempt curly hair that was almost an afro, standing many inches above his head. He has grown a short beard. His eyes were downcast most of the time. He touched his face and nose a lot. His feet remained in shackles while he sat in a relaxed slouch with his knees open throughout the 25-minute hearing. His facial expression seemed a bit weird and befuddled — quite intense, yet not quite there — perhaps a side effect of being kept in isolation for over a year. He seemed almost disoriented but maybe he was just exhausted from being hauled out of bed in the middle of the night."

During one pre-trial hearing, a marathon bombing victim waved his prosthetic leg angrily in Friedemann's face while she held a poster in support of Dzhokhar. After photos of the confrontation appeared on the news, her neighbors turned against her.

"After that day, I tried to get a haircut and the owners of my local hair salon refused me service," Friedemann told Masslive.com.

As the jury selection approached an end, CNN legal analyst and famed trial lawyer Mark Geragos said, "He looks like an impressionable Neanderthal puppy. Most people who have raised teenagers have sat across a table from this kid."

Right up to the moment O'Toole announced that 12 jurors and six alternates had been chosen, Dzhokhar seemed largely bored with the process.

He fidgeted often, thumbing through court papers but not reading them, running his hands through his beard and curly hair, flipping through Post-It notes. He spoke with his jury selection specialist and attorneys only occasionally. He rarely looked at the judge and prosecutors in the Muslim style of avoiding eye contact with authority figures.

A couple of times, his attorney, Miriam Conrad, tapped him on the shoulder to get him to pay attention.

On Tuesday, March 3, 2015, Judge O'Toole announced a jury had been chosen after interviewing 256 local residents. He scheduled opening statements in the trial to begin the next day.

The defense attorneys filed a motion to overturn the jury selection. They said the jury lacked enough minorities and young people to be a fair representation of the community. Once again, the judge denied their motion.

The jury of 10 women and eight men — six of them alternates — were mostly white but cut across all socioeconomic groups. They included an air traffic controller, a house painter, a nurse, a fashion designer, a restaurant manager, three public employees, a volunteer, and five people who were retired or unemployed.

The youngest was an auditor in his 20s, the oldest a white-haired semi-retired school bus driver.

The announcement of a jury in the Tsarnaev case came less than a week after news reports that "Jihadi John," the ISIS executioner who beheaded victims in Internet broadcasts, had been identified. Other news reports discussed a pre-trial hearing for Abd al-Rahim al-Nashiri, the accused al Qaeda mastermind of the 2000 suicide bombing of the USS Cole at the port of Aden in Yemen. The attack killed 17 American sailors and wounded 39.

He also faced the death penalty if he was convicted.

Taken together, some critics wondered whether terrorism was on trial in Boston rather than a confused young man.

THE OPENING STATEMENTS

ON THE FIRST day of the trial, Dzhokhar's lead attorney shocked everyone with an opening statement that no one expected.

"It was him," Judy Clark said as her client slouched in his chair nearby. He would not try to "sidestep" his "inexcusable" behavior that claimed the lives of three people and injured dozens, Clarke said.

However, he would ask the jury to keep his behavior in context, to remember that he did not act alone and that his domineering and violent older brother, Tamerlan, played the key role in the bombings. She entered a plea of not guilty for her client.

The bombings were "caused by a series of senseless, horribly misguided acts carried out by two brothers," Clarke said. The then-teenaged Dzhokhar was propelled on "a path borne of his brother, created by his brother and paved by his brother," the attorney said.

Much like the legal experts predicted, Clarke was not even trying to deny her client's guilt that was captured on videotape for the world to see. From the opening words of her 20-minute statement, she was trying to save him from the death penalty.

Dzhokhar was an otherwise normal teenager, Clarke said. He liked Facebook, cars and girls. His biggest mistake was his love and respect for his older brother, she said.

"The evidence will not establish and we will not argue that Tamerlan put a gun to Dzhokhar's head or that he forced him to join in the plan, but you will hear evidence about the kind of influence that this older brother had," Clarke said.

Even as he hid in a backyard boat after watching his brother get shot and run over by an SUV, Dzhokhar gave hints of Tamerlan's control over his thoughts. His scrawled writing on the side of the dry-docked boat showed "he was jealous of his brother who achieved martyrdom," Clarke said.

"It was Tamerlan who self-radicalized," she said. "It was Dzhokhar who followed."

She tried to expand on their family relationship, including Tamerlan's forceful personality and the Chechen cultural norm that implied a leadership role for the older brother. But Judge O'Toole pulled her back, cautioning her not to try to make the Tsarnaev family the primary issue. Dzhokhar was the one on trial, the judge reminded her.

Clarke asked jurors to keep an open mind, particularly during the trial's second phase when Dzhokhar would either get the death penalty or life in prison.

"It's going to be a lot to keep your hearts and minds open but that's what we ask," she said.

More than saving time and wasted energy in trying to proclaim Dzhokhar's innocence, she also had limited the most gruesome evidence against her client. There would be no need for prosecutors to present horrific stories of human tragedy to prove Dzhokhar set the bombs. His attorney already admitted, "It was him."

Now the more important issue would be what motivated him to set a bomb that killed and maimed. Was it the action of a maniac murderer or a teenager who would have preferred to drink beer in a friend's dorm room if his brother had not misled him?

Prosecutors portrayed a much different picture of Dzhokhar. He was a "terrorist" seeking revenge for U.S. military actions in the Muslim world.

As doctors tried to save the lives of bomb victims with severed limbs, Dzhokhar went shopping at a nearby Whole Foods grocery store. His primary concern seemed to be choosing a gallon of milk, said Assistant U.S. Attorney William Weinreb.

Dzhokhar "acted like he didn't have a care in the world," Weinreb said. "While victims of the bombing lay in the hospital and learned that they would have to have their limbs chopped off to save their lives, the defendant pretended that nothing had happened."

Afterward, "he hung out with friends, partied and tweeted, 'I'm a stress-free kind of guy,'" Weinreb said.

After apparently guessing the defense in advance, the prosecution tried to head off any claims of Dzhokhar's innocence being manipulated by his brother.

Dzhokhar's bomb was "the type of bombs favored by terrorists because it's designed to tear people apart and create a bloody spectacle," Weinreb said.

"He believed that he was a soldier in a holy war against Americans," Weinreb said. "He also believed that by winning that victory, he had taken a step toward reaching paradise. That was his motive for committing these crimes."

Eight-year-old Martin Richard "bled to death" from ghastly wounds while his mother watched helplessly, Weinreb said.

"The bomb tore large chunks of flesh out of Martin Richard," he said as the boy's parents sat in the courtroom.

For Lingzi Lu, 23, witnesses saw "the inside of her stomach pouring out," the prosecutor said during his 50-minute opening statement. Krystle Campbell, 29, the third person killed by the blasts, suffered "gaping holes" in her body.

"The air was filled with the smell of burning sulfur and people's screams," Weinreb said.

Weinreb then called five survivors as his first witnesses and accompanied their testimony with gruesome photos and video of them lying wounded.

Rebekah Gregory, 27, walked to the witness stand with a prosthetic left leg. "My bones were literally laying next to me on the sidewalk," she testified. Her 5-year-old son called for her but she was unable to reach out to him with her shredded arm.

Sydney Corcoran, 19, lost most of her blood after one of the bombs severed her femoral artery. "I could feel my body going tingly and I was getting increasingly cold and I knew I was dying," she said.

Weinreb called the Tsarnaev brothers "partners in crime," each of them sharing the guilt.

Further evidence of Dzhokhar's callousness came from the shootout with police in Watertown, the prosecutor said.

After throwing a pressure cooker bomb at police, he drove a stolen SUV at them at top speed "trying to mow them down," Weinreb said. "The defendant ran right over his brother and dragged his body about 50 feet down the street," he said.

On the same day attorneys presented their opening statements, a bombing victim who lost a leg despite 15 failed surgeries to save it posted an open letter on her Facebook page. The response was an outpouring of sympathy for her and her outrage against Dzhokhar.

> Dear Dzhokhar Tsarnaev,
>
> My name is Rebekah Gregory. We don't really know each other and never will. But over the last two years, I have seen your face not only in pictures, but in almost every one of my nightmares. Moments before the first blast, your stupid backpack even brushed up against my arm, but I doubt you remember because I am no one

to you. A complete stranger. And although I was merely just a blip on your radar, (someone that happened to be standing 3 feet from your designated 'good spot' for a bomb), you have been so much more to me. Because you have undoubtedly been my source of fear since April 15th, 2013. (After all, you are one of the men responsible for nearly taking my child, and for the permanent image embedded in my brain of watching someone die.) Up until now, I have been truly scared of you and because of this, fearful of everything else people might be capable of.

But today, all that changed. Because this afternoon, I got to walk into a courtroom and take my place at the witness stand, just a few feet away from where you were sitting. (I was WALKING. Did you get that?) And today I explained all the horrific details, of how you changed my life, to the people that literally hold YOURS in their hands. That's a little scary right? And this afternoon before going in, I'm not going to lie ... my palms were sweaty. And sitting up there talking to the prosecution did make me cry. But today, do you know what else happened? TODAY ... I looked at you right in the face ... and realized I wasn't afraid anymore. And today I realized that sitting across from you was somehow the crazy kind of step forward that I needed all along.

And I think that's the ironic thing that happens when someone intends something for evil. Because somehow, some way, it always ends up good. But you are a coward. A little boy who wouldn't even look me in the eyes to see that. Because you can't handle the fact that what you tried to destroy, you only made stronger. And if your eyes would've met mine for just one second, you would've also seen that what you 'blew up' really did BLOW UP. Because now you have given me (and the other survivors) a tremendous platform to help others, and essentially do our parts in changing the world for the better.

So yes ... you did take a part of me. Congratulations you now have a leg up ... literally. But in so many ways, you saved my life. Because now, I am so much more appreciative of every new day I am given. And now, I get to hug my son even tighter than before, blessed that he is THRIVING, despite everything that has happened.

So now ... while you are sitting in solitary confinement, (awaiting the verdict on your life), I will be actually ENJOYING everything this beautiful world has to offer. And guess what else? I will do so without fear ... of YOU. Because now to me you're a nobody, and it is official that you have lost. So man that really sucks for you bro. I truly hope it was worth it.

Sincerely,

Someone you shouldn't have messed with

THE PROSECUTION'S WITNESSES

IF THE DEFENSE wanted to head off heartrending stories of blood and guts by admitting Dzhokhar's guilt, the prosecution's witness list showed the strategy failed.

Many of the witnesses from March 6 onward gave accounts of personal tragedy caused by the bombs. The defense attorneys didn't even try to cross-examine the ones who gave the most pitiful testimony.

One of the first witnesses was Boston police officer Frank Chiola, who was on public safety duty during what he described as a "good day for everyone." It didn't last long.

As throngs of people screamed after the first explosion, he ran toward the site of the blast. He approached a group of victims on the ground as the second bomb exploded.

Chiola said he "saw blood everywhere. People's faces, you couldn't tell who was alive and who was dead."

He did CPR on Krystle Campbell. "She was suffering. She was in pain," he said. "From the waist down, it's really tough to describe, complete mutilation."

She died anyway.

Jeffrey Bauman, who walked into court on two prosthetic legs, testified about standing near the finish line with friends as he waited for his girlfriend to finish the race.

He told about being bumped by a young man carrying a backpack he described as a "suspicious kid." As they exchanged glances, Bauman noticed he "didn't look like he was having fun like everybody else."

As Bauman turned around again moments later, he noticed the man was gone but his backpack was lying on the ground.

"I just thought it was weird," Bauman said.

He heard his friends say they should leave but then saw a flash and heard a blast.

"It smelled like the Fourth of July ... I lifted my head and that's when I first saw the chaos behind me," Bauman said. "I could see my bones and flesh sticking out. I just went into tunnel vision. I wasn't thinking about anything but my legs at that point."

Photos of Bauman being pushed in a wheelchair by bystanders toward an ambulance became one of the most memorable images from the 2013 marathon. His legs were a bloody mess while other traces of blood smeared his face and shirt.

Of the three surgeries he underwent at Boston Medical Center, he remembered only one of them. He awoke to find his legs amputated and a breathing tube in his mouth.

He wrote a note for police saying he saw the bomber and could describe him.

"I only had one goal in my mind at that point. It was to tell whoever I could what I knew," Bauman testified.

FBI agents and state police arrived shortly afterward to collect the first description of the then-unknown bomber.

Amputation victim Roseann Sdoia testified in agonizing detail about her first realization that her right leg was gone. She was up Boylston Street when the first bomb exploded, waiting to watch a friend approach the finish line. A man to her left yelled for everyone to get in the street.

She was too short to climb over the barricade. Instead she chose to run to her right.

"I saw two flashes of white light explode at my feet," she said. "I remember, and I think it's probably before I hit the ground, but in my head, it registered that I lost my leg."

When she regained consciousness, blood poured out of her leg around her displaced kneecap.

"I was starring in a horror movie," Sdoia said. "I knew I was bleeding out and I needed to stay calm and stay conscious because if I didn't, I would die."

Two men came to her aid, one a physician's assistant, the other a Northeastern University student. They straightened her right leg, which created "excruciating" pain for her, then tightened a belt around the leg as a tourniquet to stop the bleeding.

She kept her eyes closed as she arrived at Massachusetts General Hospital, not wanting to see the tragedy that swirled around her. She awoke in the hospital later to find her leg amputated.

"There was nothing else I could do at that point," Sdoia testified.

Two of the witnesses told about seeing their children severely injured by the blasts. They described their children's bleeding bodies, not knowing whether they would live before they were taken off to hospitals for surgery.

Schoolteacher Alan Hern said he found his 11-year-old son "full blood, something seen in a war movie."

Other police and FBI agents described how they scrambled to find evidence leading them to the Tsarnaev brothers.

FBI special agent Richard Claflin talked about collecting three dozen videos from the marathon. Within days, the FBI narrowed the possibilities of suspects in the videos, first determining their exit routes from the scene of the crime, then selecting the still-unidentified "black hat" and "white hat" as the bombers.

FBI computer expert James Tyra testified that as he reviewed the videos, he spotted the smoking gun evidence.

"A person approximately five minutes before the bombing walked up to a place in front of the Forum with a backpack, casually turned and set the backpack down," Tyra said. "And then a bomb went off very shortly after that."

Defense attorneys continued to surprise by declining to cross-examine the victims with the most gruesome stories. Apparently they wanted to avoid the image of bullying people who had gained martyrdom status in the Boston area, perhaps alienating the jury.

Meanwhile, a long list of prosecution witnesses hammered away at any hope for acquittal.

The previously unidentified Chinese man who was kidnapped in his own SUV testified about how close he felt to death as the Tsarnaev brothers drove him around three days after the bombings.

Tamerlan opened the door of the leased SUV and pointed a gun "right at my head" and demanded money, said Dun Meng, a partner in a food delivery company.

Meng repeated many of his statements from his 2013 Boston Globe interview, including the quote from Tamerlan talking about the marathon bombings. "I did it and I just killed a policeman in Cambridge," Meng said as he quoted Tamerlan again.

Everything Meng had said about escaping from the SUV as the Tsarnaevs stopped for gas was supported by gas station video, which prosecutors showed the jury for the first time.

The video showed Meng running into a gas station, out of breath and obviously upset. He begged the gas station attendant to call the police, explaining in accented English that he had been carjacked.

The video shows the attendant calling 911 as Meng crawls into a storage area behind the cash register. Another video showed Dzhokhar at an ATM as he used Meng's bank card to steal his money.

After the first few days of testimony, the prosecution shifted from demonstrating the crime to showing the timeline of events leading to Dzhokhar's alleged involvement and capture.

The point behind the shift in testimony seemed to be prosecutors were trying to show Dzhokhar was a full partner in the crime, even after his domineering older brother was gone.

Police officers testified to their battle with the Tsarnaev brothers on the quiet, tree-lined residential Laurel Street in Watertown. A state trooper retold radio chatter saying, "They're throwing bombs at us. We need the bomb squad."

Then he heard another police officer report "some type of explosive and saw smoke in the street lamps."

Tamerlan tried to hurl his bombs at police like a baseball with a straight-arm throw. Dzhokhar preferred a hook shot, more like a basketball player.

The force of the blasts took on a special significance. The canister part of one pressure cooker bomb became embedded in the rear door of a parked car. One piece of shrapnel was found on the other side of a nearby house, indicating the blast blew it over the roof.

The lid of the pressure cooker was found in a child's hockey goal. Some of the shrapnel landed a block away.

Prosecutors showed jurors unexploded pipe bombs that had been filled with gunpowder and BBs. A neighbor testified he saw the Tsarnaevs trying to light a fuse and shooting guns.

In other words, the Tsarnaevs were trying to kill again.

Police testified they saw Tamerlan's gun jam and saw him throw the gun at a police sergeant. They told about rushing him, knocking him to the ground and handcuffing him.

About the same time, a witness testified, there was the sound of "an engine roar."

The SUV driven by Dzhokhar moved at high speed toward the officers. As they jumped aside, there was "a thud," the witness said. Tamerlan was dragged about 25 feet. A photograph shown to the jury showed his blood pooled in the street.

The SUV sped away but did not travel far before it was abandoned. Police found it minutes later in a neighborhood where radio and television bulletins warned residents to stay inside.

One of the residents was David Henneberry, who sometimes liked to take his private pleasure boat out for short jaunts in the ocean near Boston. As heavily armed police walked through his neighborhood, Henneberry noticed through a rear window of his house that shrink-wrap covering his boat was flapping loose in one section.

After radio and television announcers said shelter-in-place restrictions were lifted, Henneberry said he walked outside to tend to his boat cover.

Instead, he saw blood on his boat. "Not a lot but enough," Henneberry testified. A human form lay curled up in the deck of the boat, leading Henneberry to rush back into his house to call police.

Jurors were hoisted up two at a time on forklift to look inside the boat at a location near the courthouse. They saw more than a hundred bullet holes that had pierced the sides.

They also saw Dzhokhar's now-faded blood and writing on the inside of the boat. "Stop killing our innocent civilians and we will stop," the scrawled lettering said.

Stephan Silva testified about how he met his friend Dzhokhar. "I considered him one of my best friends back in the day," Silva said. He described Dzhokhar as "one of the realest and coolest kids you ever met" who was popular and a good student in high school.

He liked him enough that Silva loaned him a gun he kept hidden in the ceiling of his apartment when Dzhokhar asked for it, never imagining it might be used for a terrorist attack.

When Silva heard his friend since eighth grade was a suspect in the marathon bombings, his first impression was disbelief. "Must have been his brother that got him into it," Silva posted on Facebook.

He testified about Dzhokhar discussing Tamerlan, saying "You don't want to meet my brother."

"He said his brother was very strict, very opinionated," Silva testified. Dzhokhar warned him that Tamerlan would not like him because he is not a Muslim.

However, it was not Tamerlan who asked Silva for the 9mm Ruger P95 two months before the marathon bombings. It was Dzhokhar.

As Silva, 21, walked to the witness stand, Dzhokhar perked up and looked hard at his friend with whom he attended high school and worked as a lifeguard at the Harvard University swimming pool.

Silva wore a tan prison suit as he testified about asking Dzhokhar why he wanted the gun. He said he wanted to "rip some kids," Silva said in a reference to robbing them.

Silva later asked him to return the gun. "I wanted it back," he said. "But he just kept coming up with excuses."

Silva never smiled during his testimony, which he offered in hopes of a lighter sentence on illegal gun charges and conspiracy to distribute heroin. Dzhokhar watched Silva more intensely than the previous witnesses as they sat about 10 feet apart.

Silva gave hints of what appeared to be the beginning of anti-American sentiment growing in Dzhokhar. He recalled that Dzhokhar told a teacher, "American foreign policy tends to be hostile toward the Middle East."

He quoted Dzhokhar saying that the United States was "taking over other people's cultures and telling them what to do." Prosecutors portrayed the two high school buddies as part of a crowd that often dealt in drugs.

Jurors were shown a photograph of Dzhokhar sitting under a black flag with Arabic lettering in his family home. The flag is commonly associated with radical Islamic groups.

Prosecution witnesses left no doubt about the source of the bombs, where they were made and the materiel that went into them. FBI agents talked about a small room behind the kitchen in the Tsarnaevs' apartment cluttered with wire cutters, duct tape, glue, hobby wire and the gasket and part of a lid from a pressure cooker. In another room, FBI agents found bags of BBs and a jar of small nails.

"The mindset was these tools could be used in the making of a device," testified FBI special agent Christopher Derks. BBs "were all over the floor," he said. The investigation showed BBs were glued inside pipes in the bombs to increase the amount of shrapnel.

Credit card purchase records and store receipts showed Tamerlan started collecting bomb-making equipment early in 2013.

A Jan. 31, 2013 purchase from the Macy's department store in Saugus showed Tamerlan purchased two pressure cookers. One of them held six quarts and the second held four quarts.

Remnants of the bombs showed the pressure cooker brand as Fagor Elite, which is sold exclusively by Macy's. The pressure cooker bomb that exploded at the marathon finish line held six quarts. The one that exploded up the street held four quarts.

On Feb. 8, 2013, Tamerlan bought a remote control automobile transmitter and a battery from an Internet retailer called Nitro RCX for $175. He used his email address, Chechen_style@yahoo.com, for the purchase. FBI agents said the same remote control transmitter detonated the marathon bombs.

A note in Tamerlan's wallet listed the address of a Walmart in New Hampshire, where store receipts showed he purchased boxes of BBs on March 6, 2013.

On another day, Dzhokhar and his brother were shown on video arriving and leaving from a shooting range in New Hampshire. They rented two 9mm handguns and purchased ammunition for a total of $170. The guns and ammo were similar to the gun used during their shootout with police.

On a form required by the Manchester Firing Range on March 20, 2013, both brothers listed their shooting ability as "intermediate." They also said they did not smoke marijuana and had no history of mental illness.

Tamerlan's fingerprints later were found on the Ruger 9mm handgun fired at police in Watertown. Dzhokhar's fingerprints were found on the pellet gun left at the scene.

The day before the marathon bombings, Tamerlan was filmed by surveillance cameras at the Watertown Target. Receipts were found in his wallet for purchases of two backpacks at the store, one for $39.99 and the other for $59.99.

To demonstrate the extent of the threat from Dzhokhar in his alleged role as a terrorist, prosecutors called Matthew Levitt, a senior fellow at the Washington Institute for Near East Studies.

Dzhokhar's Twitter posts and scrawled handwriting inside the boat where he hid showed strong radical Islamic influence, Levitt said. They were typical of "al-Awlaki's statements and other writings from the radicalizers," Levitt testified.

Awlaki was the al Qaeda propaganda chief killed by a U.S. drone strike in 2011.

The marathon bombings could be interpreted as part of a "global jihad movement" that incited Muslims to strike violently at the United States, Levitt said.

Further evidence of Dzhokhar's threat were revealed in his text messages.

A November 2012 message to a friend said the U.S. presidential election was a waste because "killing muslims is the only promise they will fulfill."

A December 2012 text message to a friend said, "I wanna bring justice for my people."

A Jan. 28, 2013 message from Dzhokhar to a friend said he was considering an option to achieve the "Highest level of Jannah" or paradise in Islamic terms. "I got a plan I'll tell yu later about it," he wrote.

Most of the prosecution's case was presented with the professionalism that would be expected of top-tier federal prosecutors. If they made a mistake, it was when they told jurors about the contents of Dzhokhar's laptop, desktop computer and iPod. They contained propaganda from radical Muslim cleric Anwar al-Awlaki and al Qaeda's online magazine "Inspire."

Although prosecutors intended to prove Dzhokhar's violent Islamic tendencies, they opened the door for defense attorneys to show Tamerlan's influence over his younger brother.

Defense attorney William Fick dug his heels into an FBI computer specialist who he accused of misrepresenting the files found in Dzhokhar's computer. FBI special agent Kevin Swindon mentioned a few bits of information about radical Islam but he left out other files on pop music and homework, Fick said.

Swindon appeared flustered under the aggressive questioning.

Fick implied the radical Islamic information was downloaded by Tamerlan onto an external hard drive then transferred to other mobile devices. The hard drive was found near Tamerlan's body.

One of the Inspire magazine articles was entitled, "How to Make a Bomb in the Kitchen of Your Mom." It included a statement saying, "Can I make an effective bomb that causes damage to the enemy from ingredients available in any kitchen in the world? The answer is yes. But before how, we ask why? It is because Allah says ... every Muslim is required to defend his religion and his nation."

Other downloads in the Tsarnaevs' laptop included audio files from Awlaki's lectures and a book entitled "Join the Caravan" by Imam Abdullah Azzam, a founder of al Qaeda.

"Are you aware that that hard drive recovered in Watertown was formatted by Tamerlan Tsarnaev," Fisk asked.

"I don't have information to confirm that," Swindon said.

Fisk also asked, "Did you ever become aware in your role that every single file and folder on this hard drive was created by Tamerlan Tsarnaev's computer?"

"No," Swindon replied.

"Was anyone else at the FBI aware of that," Fisk asked.

"Not that I know of," Swindon replied.

Other times, Fick tried to demonstrate what appeared to be the FBI's ignorance or lapses in gathering evidence.

"Are you aware it was easy [for the FBI] to get into Tamerlan's encrypted files because he had an easy password," Fisk asked.

"I was not aware of that," Swindon replied.

Dzhokhar's use of the family computer was not targeted as directly at radical Islam, Fick said. Dzhokhar and his sister, Bella, would use tame web sites like Skype, Facebook and the Russian version of Facebook, called VK. One of his top search terms was Chechnya, the family's original homeland.

"Would you agree that the top two search terms, you wouldn't be surprised to find them in the computer search terms of an adolescent male," Fisk asked.

"I'm not an adolescent psychologist," Swindon replied.

"Are you aware that among the top 16 search terms, none of the terms are 'Islam' or 'jihad,'" Fisk asked.

Prosecutors objected successfully to the question before Swindon answered.

Prosecutors tried to show that although Tamerlan was the prime mover for the bomb plot, his brother was a willing participant.

One witness quoted Dzhokhar talking about Tamerlan,

saying, "He's very influential." Dzhokhar also allegedly said, "He's a role model for us."

The testimony played directly into the strategy of the defense team. They did not dispute that Dzhokhar participated in the bombings. They were arguing that Tamerlan's "influential" and "role model" status for Dzhokhar meant the younger brother was led astray but he was not the evil villain.

Defense attorneys succeeded in shifting much of the blame to Tamerlan, but the bigger question was whether it would convince the jury to spare Dzhokhar's life.

The prosecution had one last shot at Dzhokhar before resting their case. And it was devastating.

They called Dr. Henry Nields, the Massachusetts chief medical examiner. He brought with him photos of 8-year-old Martin Richard after his body was mangled by the second pressure cooker bomb. Dzhokhar was the one who set the bomb.

The boy's body was lacerated in his liver and left kidney. His left arm was torn off, his spine severed, his stomach was ruptured and exposed. He suffered third-degree burns that changed the color of some of his skin.

Martin's parents sat stone-faced in the second row. Bill Richard held his wife with his arm around her shoulder.

As they looked at photos of the deceased child, at least three of the jurors wiped their eyes with tissue as they wept.

Meanwhile, Nields described removing nails, BBs, splinters of wood and black plastic from Martin's body. He held up his bloodstained clothing.

Another photograph showed Martin Richard standing on the base of a barricade next to his sister as they watched the marathon runners. Dzhokhar is standing only a few feet behind them.

Defense attorneys showed photographs with other people standing between Dzhokhar and the children at different moments before the blast. They were trying to show he was not targeting the Richard children.

But it still was not Tamerlan in the photos. It was Dzhokhar.

The final sentence of the prosecution's case came from Nields, who responded to a question about Martin's age. "He was 8 years old," he said.

THE DEFENSE TRIES ITS BEST

THE DEFENSE STARTED presenting its case on March 30, 2015. From the start of their two-day presentation, defense attorneys were trying to limit the damage from the prosecution. They had no chance of winning an acquittal.

Defense attorneys called only four witnesses and questioned them for a total of five hours compared with 92 witnesses over 15 days for the prosecution. Their entire case was designed to prove the Svengali defense, which means someone influenced someone else to commit a crime. In Dzhokhar's case, his attorneys tried to show Tamerlan was the culprit, not his younger brother.

Dzhokhar's entry into the courtroom was greeted with the usual tapping on cellphones as reporters and onlookers sent Tweets about how he was dressed and any mannerisms he showed. There was not much to report. Dzhokhar leaned back in his chair occasionally, scratched his nose, stroked his beard and spoke with his attorney. He showed very little emotion as he sat nearly in the center of Courtroom Nine. His attorneys, Miriam Conrad and Judy Clarke, sat on either side of him.

The defense's prime witness was an FBI agent who described how investigators catalogued evidence. It revealed that Tamerlan downloaded extremist Islamic propaganda onto Dzhokhar's laptop. Tamerlan researched how to make a bomb and acquire the components. Tamerlan's fingerprints were found on shrapnel at the marathon finish line and on a soldering iron used to assemble the bombs.

While Tamerlan was in Saugus buying pressure cookers for bomb casings, Dzhokhar's cellphone records showed he was in New Bedford. While Tamerlan was in New Hampshire buying BBs for bomb shrapnel, Dzhokhar never left Massachusetts.

Prosecutors had showed jihadi propaganda was found on Dzhokhar's computer, but it was transferred from Tamerlan's laptop, according to defense witness Mark Spencer, a digital forensics expert.

Other activity logged on Tamerlan's laptop showed he researched Ruger handguns, similar to the one used to kill police officer Sean Collier in Watertown. Tamerlan also searched for information on fireworks and on model car components that can be used as detonators. His search terms included "transmitter and receiver," and "fireworks firing system."

No similar searches were logged on Dzhokhar's computer, Spencer testified. Instead, his computer searches typically included Facebook, a Russian social media site and a porn web site, similar to many teenagers who have no Islamic holy war ambitions.

Other defense evidence to show Dzhokhar was as human as the kid next door was a letter he wrote to University of Massachusetts at Dartmouth administrators three months before the bombings. He asked them to renew his financial aid despite a failing grade point average of 1.09.

"This year I lost too many of my loved relatives," Dzhokhar wrote. "I was unable to cope with the stress and maintain school work. I am at the point where I am finally able to focus on my school work. I wish to do well so one day I can help those in need in my country, especially my family members."

The college administrators denied his request.

The defense tried to bolster their case with testimony from FBI fingerprint analyst Elaina Graff. They succeeded in getting Graff to say Tamerlan's fingerprints were found on components of the bombs that exploded on Boylston Street. They included a transmitter, a pressure cooker lid, a jar of nails, a caulking gun, rolls of duct tape and the soldering iron.

Evidence of Dzhokhar's fingerprints on the shrapnel, the tools or anything else associated with the bombs was minimal.

One exception was a plastic container that contained three pounds of explosive powder. Six sets of Tamerlan's fingerprints were found on it and two sets from Dzhokhar.

Some bomb components and the backpacks carried by the brothers held no fingerprints, Graff testified. "Fingerprints are very fragile," she said. They could have been wiped off or evaporated.

Prosecutor William Weinreb largely discredited the fingerprint evidence that pointed almost exclusively to Tamerlan. Weinreb showed that heat from the explosions could destroy fingerprints. In addition, Tamerlan might have had sweaty hands that are more likely to leave fingerprints than dry hands.

Fingerprints alone were inconclusive because "the bombs didn't build themselves, the backpacks didn't carry themselves," Weinreb said. "The presence of fingerprints tells you he touched it but the absence of a person's fingerprints doesn't tell you whether he did or didn't touch it."

On Tuesday, March 31, lead defense attorney Judy Clarke stood and said the defense rested.

Judge O'Toole told jurors to return the following Monday for closing arguments. He reminded them not to discuss the case with anyone, "including to yourself in the mirror."

"People will want to know things," he said. "You can't tell them."

"Nothing. Please," he said.

During closing arguments, the prosecution summarized the evidence with a stinging critique of Dzhokhar's involvement in the bombings. He was a cold-blooded killer and a terrorist who embraced the rhetoric of Islamic militant propaganda, according to Assistant U.S. Attorney Aloke Chakravarty.

"He wanted to wake the mujahedeen, the holy warrior, so he chose Patriots Day," Chakravarty told jurors. "The marathon day. A day when the eyes of the world would be on Boston."

The prosecutor pointed at Dzhokhar as he said, "He wanted to tell the world why he did it and he wanted to take credit. He wanted to justify it."

Chakravarty's more than hour-long closing argument retold the horror of William Richard watching his battered son die. "His entire body was shattered," the prosecutor said. "It was broken, eviscerated, burned. There wasn't a part of this boy's body that wasn't destroyed."

He showed a video of the victims lying bleeding at the finish line. One of them was graduate student Lingzi Lu. A friend described a hole blown through her leg.

"The defendant killed her too," Chakravarty said.

He discussed Dzhokhar's presence when Officer Collier was killed, when businessman Dun Meng was kidnapped in his own SUV and the pressure cooker bomb he threw at police during the shootout in Watertown.

Massachusetts Bay Transportation Authority Officer Richard Donohue was hit by friendly fire and seriously injured during the shootout. Chakravarty said "that chain of events would not have happened and Officer Donohue would not have been injured" if not for the Tsarnaev brothers.

Even as he hid from police in a backyard boat, Dzhokhar clung to his radical politics as he wrote, "Stop killing our innocent people and we will stop" in the side of the boat.

"He is negotiating the terms of death with America,"

Chakravarty said. "This is what the defendant is thinking after all this."

Chakravarty ended his speech with a multimedia presentation that included a chant, or nasheed, downloaded onto Dzhokhar's electronic devices. The nasheed was associated with Anwar al-Awlaki, the al Qaeda propagandist.

As the musical chant played, gruesome video and photos from the marathon bombings were displayed on monitors. "They thought they were soldiers," Chakravarty said. "They thought they were mujahedeen and they would bring their battle to Boston. He thought his cause was more important than the people around him."

When Clarke took her turn during the closing arguments, she again invoked her client's age, his naïveté and his domineering older brother as facts that should diminish his blame. She did not deny Dzhokhar set one of the bombs that killed and wounded innocent people.

"In the past few weeks, we have come face-to-face with tragedy, suffering and grief in dimensions none of us could imagine," Clarke said. "We've heard words, we've heard screams and we've heard cries. For this suffering and pain, there is no excuse."

She sometimes described Dzhokhar as an "adolescent," a "kid" and a "teenager." "Tamerlan led and [Dzhokhar] followed," Clarke said.

"We don't deny that Dzhokhar fully participated in the events, but if not for Tamerlan, it would not have happened," Clarke said in her 45-minute final plea before the jury deliberated.

While Dzhokhar was at school, Tamerlan was at Walmart and Target buying bomb-making materials. Tamerlan was the one who shot Officer Collier, not Dzhokhar.

"They're both different people who thought differently, acted differently and had a different role in the conspiracy," Clarke said.

She accused prosecutors of exaggerating Dzhokhar's role. Yes, Dzhokhar did set his backpack bomb behind children, but they were not the target, Clarke said. Instead, Dzhokhar had randomly picked a spot near a tree.

"It doesn't make it better but let's not make his intent any worse than it was," the defense attorney said. She told the jury, "we're not asking you to go easy on Dzhokhar. The crimes deserve to be condemned and the time is now."

But she added, "We ask you to hold your minds open ... to what more there is to hear, what more there is to learn, what more there is to understand."

Assistant U.S. Attorney William Weinreb delivered the prosecution's 15-minute rebuttal. He said the defense was trying to help Dzhokhar blame a dead man for his own actions.

"It's an effort to keep trying to point the finger at someone else," Weinreb said. "The defendant and his brother were full partners. They were equally guilty."

Evidence of Dzhokhar's approval of the bombings was found in his behavior afterward, even as ambulances carted victims from the scene, Weinreb said.

"If you are capable of such hate, such callousness that you can murder and maim 20 people and then drive to Whole Foods to buy some milk, can you really blame it on your brother?" he asked.

He referred to the murder of Officer Collier when he said, "They knew exactly what they were going to do. They must have planned it ahead of time. It was a coldblooded execution."

He also emphasized that Dzhokhar was dedicated to radical Islam, rather than having a passing, juvenile interest in the subject.

"He believed in it enough to murder people," Weinreb said.

On April 7, the jury began deliberating. By the next day, after 11 hours of deliberations, they reached a verdict.

The courtroom fell silent as a clerk stood in the well of

Courtroom Nine and read the verdicts on each of 30 criminal charges. The room was packed with bombing survivors, their families and journalists. None of Dzhokhar's family was present.

"Guilty," the clerk said after reading the first charge. "Guilty," she said on the second charge. "Guilty" on the third and all the way through to the 30th.

In other words, the jury was resoundingly convinced by the prosecution's argument that Dzhokhar Tsarnaev was a full partner in planting the Boston Marathon bombs.

During the 25-minute roll call on the verdicts, Dzhokhar stood expressionless, his arms folded or clasped at times. He wore a dark jacket and gray shirt. Clarke stood to his left, turning pages of her copy of the verdict on the table in front of them as the clerk read it. Dzhokhar looked down at the pages.

After the clerk finished reading, Judge O'Toole explained to jurors the trial would next move to the penalty phase. They were still "an active jury, subject to your oath," he told them. They should continue avoiding discussion about the case.

The onlookers shuffled out of the courtroom.

Boston Mayor Martin J. Walsh issued a statement shortly afterward saying, "I hope today's verdict provides a small amount of closure for the survivors, families and all impacted by the violent and tragic events surrounding the 2013 Boston Marathon. The incidents of those days have forever left a mark on our city."

Another response came from Dzhokhar's mother, Zubeidat, who posted a note to a family friend on a Russian social media site calling Americans "terrorists."

"I will never forget it," she wrote. "May God bless those who helped my son. The terrorists are the Americans and everyone knows it. My son is the best of the best."

Bombing survivor Karen Brassard told members of the media that Dzhokhar received the punishment he deserved. "He was all in," she reportedly said. "He's a grown man and made choices knowing what the outcome could be."

The trial answered the question of Dzhokhar's guilt. It did nothing to figure out why the FBI missed clues that might have stopped the marathon bombings. It also gave no hint the guilty verdict would prevent other lone wolf attacks.

The trial reinforced what was believed from the first about the Tsarnaev brothers, namely that they are classic examples of people who feel disenfranchised from society seeking to become something greater through terrorism.

They were not recruited as soldiers by a larger organization or even paid mercenaries. They were lured to set off bombs by a combination of their own feelings of inadequacy and a desire to be part of the glorious international movement of Islamic extremism. The war on terror elevated extremism from the lunatic fringe of international politics to an appealing adventure for the world's young Muslims.

Various government reports analyzed what went wrong to create the mess of the marathon bombings. None of them pinpointed a problem that could be resolved easily.

Days before the verdict, the Commonwealth of Massachusetts released its "After Action Report" that critiqued the emergency response. The police endured mild criticism for being disorganized in parts of their effort. So many patrol cars clogged the streets near the Watertown shootout that police were unable to chase Dzhokhar immediately as he escaped. The report overlooked lingering questions about where the bombs were built and the FBI's failure to spot the threat from Tamerlan.

A March 2014 U.S. House Homeland Security Committee report basically repeated news reports. It was most notable for complaints by federal agencies that blamed each other for failing to cooperate in compiling information for the report.

Inspectors general from the CIA, the Justice Department and Homeland Security Department released a report in April 2014. They blamed Russian security agencies for failing to notify

U.S. agencies about Tamerlan's radical Islamic tendencies.

Several members of Congress traveled to Russia to get answers about why the Russians did not notify U.S. intelligence services. They received a briefing at the U.S. Embassy in Moscow but returned with nothing enlightening.

The only obvious conclusion was that identifying and stopping lone wolf terrorists is difficult and will not end soon.

A LIFE ON THE LINE

THE FINAL COURT procedure to decide whether Dzhokhar's life would be spared started on April 21 against a backdrop chock-full of hot-blooded politics.

Days earlier, on April 15, Bostonians marked the two-year anniversary of the bombings with a mournful ceremony at the finish line of the marathon.

As bagpipes played, Massachusetts' governor unveiled commemorative banners on light poles. The orange banners displayed a white heart with a road receding into it and the word "Boston."

At 2:49 p.m., the time of the first detonation, the crowd stood silently for a moment of silence. Church bells tolled throughout the city.

At the nearby Old South Church, Rev. Demetrios Tonias, dean of the Annunciation Greek Orthodox Cathedral led an interfaith service attended by hundreds of people.

"We turn now to acknowledge that life goes on," Tonias said. "Living goes on. Our prayers go on. Our grief goes on. But so, too, does our resiliency go on."

The next day, mourning turned to outrage again when an American Muslim from Ohio was charged with plotting a lone wolf attack against a U.S. military base.

Abdiraham Sheik Mohamud, 23, was allegedly trained by an al Qaeda affiliate organization in Syria before returning to his home in Columbus. He reportedly told a person unnamed in the indictment that he wanted to do something "big," which could include killing American soldiers at a Texas military base "execution style."

He was charged with three felonies in federal court.

Threats against the United States were nothing new. But a homegrown terrorist, with the same elusive potential for striking a deathblow as the Tsarnaev brothers, once again inflamed public anger.

Meanwhile, behind-the-scenes speculation continued about what the seven-woman, five-man jury that convicted Dzhokhar Tsarnaev after less than 12 hours of deliberation would give him for a sentence.

Life in prison or death by injection?

The Boston Globe weighed in with an editorial that mirrored its state's long-held opinion of the death penalty.

"Even supporters of the death penalty should have some qualms about putting Dzhokhar Tsarnaev to death," the Globe's editorial board wrote. "Sentencing Tsarnaev to death would ensure endless appeals, substitute vengeance for justice and risk letting him become a martyr."

Life imprisonment was a "no-brainer" better option than execution, the editorial said.

"Tsarnaev was 19 at the time of the bombing; he was apparently a heavy drug user; he had no prior criminal record," the editors wrote. "By themselves, none of these would seem like a particularly good reason to spare him, but taken as a whole ... they should plant seeds of doubt."

The editorial concluded by saying, "Tsarnaev obviously should spend the rest of his life in prison. His defense has already made a good case that he does not meet the exceptionally high standards for a federal execution."

To the surprise of everyone, Martin Richard's family penned an open letter to the Justice Department that was printed on the front page of The Boston Globe, agreeing the death penalty would be inappropriate.

A death penalty would lead to years of appeals and keep public attention focused Dzhokhar, forcing the Richards' two surviving children "to grow up with the lingering, painful reminder of what the defendant took from them," the letter said. "As long as the defendant is in the spotlight, we have no choice but to live a story told on his terms, not ours. The minute the defendant fades from our newspapers and TV screens is the minute we begin the process of rebuilding our lives and our family."

Some Boston Globe readers e-mailed letters to the editor strongly disagreeing with the calls for mercy.

"Get Sparky ready," a reader who signed himself as Sunday@1 wrote in a reference to the electric chair.

Another reader using the name Skipper2115 wrote that he was a death penalty opponent "my entire life" until Dzhokhar Tsarnaev came to trial.

"He placed the bomb on the ground next to a 8 year old boy and his family ... He walked away with a smug look and bought milk."

However, death penalty advocates were a minority in Boston. A poll taken after the guilty verdict by local public radio station WBUR showed 61 percent of residents preferred life in prison for Dzhokhar. Only 26 percent supported the death penalty.

A National Public Radio poll showed 62 percent of Boston residents opposed the death penalty for Dzhokhar while 27 percent supported it.

The statistics for Boston were different than much of the United States. An NBC television poll found 47 percent of Americans said he should be executed. Forty-two percent wanted him to get life in prison. Eleven percent were uncertain.

In pro-death penalty Texas, a poll found 63 percent of Texans wanted the death penalty for Dzhokhar while 33 percent opposed it.

On April 20, 2015, the Boston Marathon went off without hitch. Security was tighter than most years but the most unusual part of the marathon was the guessing about whether Dzhokhar would get the death penalty.

Absent from the festivities were the 12 jurors and six alternates, who Judge O'Toole had forbidden from showing up. He was concerned their attendance could influence their opinion.

Lelisa Desisa of Ethiopia won the race in two hours and nine minutes on the cool and drizzly day but few people paid attention as participants' thoughts turned to the sentencing phase of Dzhokhar's trial.

The next day, federal prosecutor Nadine Pelligrini rose in Courtroom Nine to tell the jury, "Jahar Tsarnaev was and is unrepentant, uncaring and untouched by the havoc and sorrow that he has created. He was willing to cross every line for glory and reward."

Killing people at the marathon was bad enough but the way he did it made the crime unforgivable, according to the prosecutor. The victims suffered searing pain, 17 of them with limbs blown off and others with life-altering injuries.

Pelligrini held up photos of the three deceased bombing victims and Officer Collier.

"All had rich and fulfilling lives; now these beautiful faces are memories," she said. "They are symbols of loss."

She also held up a photo of Dzhokhar in a holding cell three months after the marathon bombings. It shows him with his middle finger raised in an act of defiance.

"Jahar Tsarnaev was determined and destined to be America's worst nightmare," Pelligrini told the jury. "His heart was full of rage."

The first victim impact statement came from Celeste Corcoran, who had parts of both legs amputated because of bomb injuries. She was waiting for her sister near the finish line when the bombs exploded.

"I, unfortunately, remember every single detail," Corcoran said. There was the concussion of the blast, choking on smoke, hearing "blood-curdling screams" and the image of severely injured people.

"I remember looking around and seeing blood everywhere," Corcoran testified. "I remember thinking ... 'No, this has to stop, this couldn't be real.'"

Prosecutors showed new video and photos of the screaming victims moments after the blast. Dzhokhar remained stone-faced at the defense table.

William Campbell Jr., the father of deceased bombing victim Krystle Campbell, testified that he called his daughter "Princess."

"I never called her Krystle," he said. "I miss my hug every day. I miss that most."

Several jurors wept openly during parts of the sentencing hearing as they listened to the most heart-wrenching stories.

One of them came from Adrienne Haslet-Davis, who started crying as she described coming to Boylston Street to watch the marathon but leaving by dragging herself on her stomach into a restaurant. One of her legs, much of which was amputated later at a hospital, was covered with blood.

At the hospital, "I just kept screaming I was a ballroom dancer," she testified. She assumed, incorrectly, that her husband was dead.

And on it went for three days of the prosecution's case seeking the death penalty. Victim after victim or their relatives talking about the injuries and the heartache that followed.

Steve Woolfenden talked about lying on the sidewalk, still hot from the explosion, with his left leg blown off below the knee. He tried to pull his 3-year-old son out of the stroller next to him but his fingers were numb.

His son yelled, "Mommy, Daddy," over and again, despite a piece of shrapnel in his skull that made blood drip from the left side of his head.

"I was completely terrified because I didn't know if I was ever going to see my son again," said Woolfenden, a biomedical researcher. "There was blood all over the sidewalk, all around me."

He described Martin Richard weakly raising his hands a final time as his mother leaned over her dying son, saying, "Martin, please."

Marc Fucarile talked about spending 100 days in a hospital after losing his right leg. Most of the skin from his back was cut away at different times to graft onto other parts of his body.

"They slice your skin off then spread it out using almost like a pizza dough roller," he testified.

His medical treatment continued two years after the bombings to save his left leg. As he testified, he was taking about 70 pills per day of various medications.

David King, a Massachusetts General Hospital trauma surgeon who ran in the 2013 marathon, said the wounds he treated after rushing to the hospital reminded him of injuries he saw among injured soldiers as a combat surgeon in Iraq and Afghanistan.

The message from the victims' and witnesses' testimony was clear. No one who could so heartlessly inflict such severe injury on innocent persons deserved to breathe the same air as them.

THE DEFENSE'S LAST-DITCH EFFORT

THE DEFENSE OPENED its final plea for Dzhokhar's life with David Bruck, one of his attorneys, acknowledging to jurors the horrendous suffering the marathon bombs inflicted.

But did they also understand the influence of his brother over the impressionable young man?

"If Tamerlan hadn't been in the picture, would Jahar have done this on his own," Bruck asked.

Tamerlan was the one absorbed by revenge against Americans for their wars against Islamic fighters in Iraq and Afghanistan. "What Tamerlan's computer shows is obsession," Bruck said. "He was consumed by jihad. It had become almost all he did and all he thought about."

But it was too late to punish him, to try for an "evening of the scales," the attorney said. Tamerlan was dead, leaving only the teenaged brother.

Dzhokhar "was a good kid" caught up in a troubled family. The death penalty would resolve nothing and probably turn him into a martyr for Muslim terrorists. A better option would be life in prison, where he would disappear into obscurity, never again to grab headlines or disrupt the peace-of-mind of anyone else.

Bruck showed the jury an aerial image of the U.S. Penitentiary Administrative Maximum Facility in Florence, Colorado, where Dzhokhar would spend 23 hours a day in solitary confinement.

"He goes here and he's forgotten," Bruck said. "No more spotlight, like the death penalty brings."

He asked the jury to consider the tempestuous road that led Dzhokhar to the marathon bombings. His family were Chechens first driven from their homeland by Stalin in the 1940s, displaced to various sites as ethnic strife continued in Russia before making their way to Cambridge, Massachusetts.

Dzhokhar's mother "turned to fundamentalist religion" as her dreams for a better life in the United States dissolved, finally divorcing her husband, then moving back to Russia. Dzhokhar was left in the care of his domineering, radical older brother.

Dzhokhar "was a lost teenager with very little motivation to do anything on his own," his attorney said.

The defense called Judith Russell, Tamerlan's mother-in-law, as a witness. Islam "became a sort of, I don't know, obsession" for Tamerlan, she said.

He made a "selfish" six-month trip to Russia in 2012 and returned as a radical Muslim, his mother-in-law said. His constant babble on politics was "annoying" but "he had a certain charm," she said.

He exerted an influence over the religious and political beliefs of his wife, Katherine, similar to Dzhokhar. "She hadn't been religious as a child," her mother said. The change became obvious when she purchased a book titled "Islam for Dummies."

A computer expert testified that Katherine did research on her computer about the rewards in heaven for the wife of a martyr to Islam. Search terms more than a year before the bombings included, "rewards for wife of mujahedeen" and "if your husband becomes a shahid, what are the rewards for you?"

On the day of the bombings, Katherine texted a friend who

was checking in on her by writing, "A lot more people are killed every day in Syria and in other places." In another text she wrote, "Innocent people."

The personality differences between Tamerlan and Dzhokhar were obvious even as they were being transported by ambulance to Beth Israel Deaconess Medical Center. Paramedics testified that Tamerlan tried to escape from his ambulance stretcher and shouted at them as they tried to put an IV in his arm.

Dzhokhar responded to questions, moved his legs when he was asked and informed paramedics he was allergic to cats. He did not struggle when paramedics removed his handcuffs so they could administer an IV.

Paramedic Laura Lee said that when the ambulance carrying Dzhokhar arrived at Beth Israel, "He asked where his brother was." Another paramedic answered that "he would find out soon," Lee testified.

John Curran, a former boxing coach for Tamerlan, testified that Dzhokhar would follow his brother to the gym, beginning when he was 10 or 11 years old. Dzhokhar was "like a puppy following his brother," the boxing coach said.

Also testifying was Catheryn Charner-Laird, Dzhokhar's third-grade teacher, who testified he "always wanted to do the right thing."

He was 9 years old in 2002 when he was Charner-Laird's student at Cambridgeport School, where he sometimes struggled with a language barrier.

"He was incredibly hardworking," the teacher said. "He cared a lot about his studies."

Charner-Laird was one of the first defense witnesses to describe how Dzhokhar's childhood as a diligent student and good-natured buddy to his friends was vastly different from the monster who planted a bomb at the marathon.

Becki Norris, Dzhokhar's seventh- and eighth-grade teacher at Community Charter School of Cambridge, seconded her testimony. She testified he was "a really hard-working, smart kid" with a bright future.

Equally interesting was what she did when she arrived home after testifying. She wrote on her Facebook page, "Over the past two years, I've discovered the painful truth that when you care deeply for someone, that doesn't stop even if they do unfathomably horrible things. Yes, he did the unforgivable. And yes, I still love him. And – this one is hard to fathom, I know – he still needs love."

She wrote her message under a photo from years earlier that showed the baby-faced Dzhokhar holding her infant daughter.

Another character witness was Alexa Guevara, who testified about Dzhokhar's "Bro Night" gatherings with friends. During spring break two years earlier, the friends shot off fireworks along the banks of the Charles River. Dzhokhar brought the fireworks in his backpack.

Dzhokhar danced through the sparks. "He was being really silly," the 21-year-old Guevara testified.

She started sobbing as she stepped off the witness stand. People in the courtroom could hear her from the hallway as she wept for her incriminated friend.

His attorneys showed the jury photos of Dzhokhar as a child with his family. One of them featured an angelic little boy with the 16-year-old Tamerlan sitting next to him on a bench. Another showed Dzhokhar smiling with his mother and sisters.

Any happy days for the Tsarnaev family were not obvious during their return to Boston from Russia. As they waited to testify, 16 FBI agents guarded them.

Dzhokhar's mother and four other relatives originally checked in to a downtown hotel but were moved by the FBI to undisclosed locations to protect them from the media and curiosity-seekers.

On Monday, May 4, Dzhokhar's aunt, Patimat Suleimanova, took the witness stand ... and Dzhokhar cried.

For the first time since his trial started, Dzhokhar dropped his impassive demeanor and wiped tears from his eyes with a tissue. Not even a judgment of guilty on all counts including murder could drive away Dzhokhar's detached attitude. But his aunt, sitting 10 feet away, stammering through her name, year and place of birth, were more than he could bear.

The stout, 65-year-old woman started sobbing uncontrollably. Judge O'Toole interrupted after several minutes to suggest the defense call a different witness until Patimat Suleimanova could compose herself.

A cousin of Dzhokhar testified earlier he was so gentle as a child that he cried while watching "The Lion King."

"He was a sunny child," Raisat Suleimanova said through a Russian interpreter. "If you looked at him, you would want to smile, even if you didn't feel good at that time."

She also said, "I think that his kindness made everybody around him kind."

A prosecutor asked Suleimanova whether bombing innocent people was an act of kindness. The defense objected and she did not answer.

After Dzhokhar's relatives testified about his history as a good and loving child, the defense turned to the "abuse excuse."

The abuse excuse refers to a criminal law strategy in which a defendant argues that his history of being abused lessens his blame for a crime. Most commonly it refers to child abuse or sexual assault. It also can mean a defendant suffers a psychological syndrome leading to irrational behavior.

The U.S. Supreme Court has ruled that defendants can present any evidence at trial that could affect their sentences. Some legal scholars, such as Harvard Law School professor Alan Dershowitz, have called the abuse excuse a "lawless invitation to vigilantism."

Examples include the 1992 case of Lorena Bobbitt, who cut off her husband's penis with a kitchen knife while he slept. She was acquitted by reason of temporary insanity after arguing her husband sexually assaulted and verbally abused her.

In Dzhokhar's case, his attorneys tried to show his father was mentally ill, leading his vile and overbearing brother to fill in as a father figure.

The defense called Dr. Alexander Niss, a psychiatrist who treated Anzor Tsarnaev from 2003 to 2005. Dzhokhar's father suffered from post-traumatic stress disorder, anxiety, seizures, paranoia and auditory hallucinations, the psychiatrist said. He took several medications to control his condition.

Anzor's illnesses made it difficult for him to work, to support his family. He made frequent emergency room visits, Niss said. He said the Russian government had tortured him but other reports cast doubt on his story.

"He had a lot of physical problems," Niss said. "He was putting his head very often on the table."

A Princeton University professor specializing in Russian and Middle Eastern history and culture testified that when the father in a Chechen family cannot lead a family, the eldest brother takes over. Younger children are expected to be obedient.

However, Tamerlan was not the compassionate role model Dzhokhar needed, according to his attorneys.

His bullying tendencies were unmistakable from the way he treated his wife, friends of Katherine Russell said. On one occasion after they had sex, he told her he had AIDS, and then laughed as she cried. Other times Russell's roommates reported loud arguments between Tamerlan and his wife.

The point was clear: Tamerlan was stubborn and demanding, occasionally even to his younger brother.

A family friend who ran a video store said she once saw Tamerlan say something "very powerful" to Dzhokhar, as if he were ordering him to wait in their car.

Dzhokhar's former brother-in-law testified about how Tamerlan became the family's decision-maker as their father struggled with his personal demons.

"There is a saying we have in Chechnya: In a family with seven sons, it is better to be a dog than the younger son," said Elmirza Khozhugov, the former husband of Ailina Tsarnaeva. "The youngest of the boys is obliged to do the things the older boys tell him."

The relationship between Tamerlan and Dzhokhar was driven by mutual respect but still allowed the older brother to dominate, Khozhugov said.

Dzhokhar "listened to Tamerlan," Khozhugov said over live video from the U.S. Embassy in Kazakhstan. "He went along any time Tamerlan would say, 'Let's go do this and that,'" Khozhugov said. "He would just go along and always find time to actually go along."

Earlier, a neuroscientist testified the "immature brain" of a 19-year-old like Dzhokhar might make him more easily led than most adults. He might not fully consider the consequences of his actions, the doctor said.

After nearly five-dozen witnesses testified about Dzhokhar being a good-hearted but misguided young man, defense attorneys again tried to convince jurors that a life sentence would be an abundantly severe sentence for his crimes.

The U.S. Penitentiary Administrative Maximum Facility in Florence, Colorado – also known as supermax – would limit him to two 15-minute phone calls with his family each month. He would be alone in a cell 23 hours per day and all his mail would be screened.

A defense team consultant on the prison system said the supermax prison was "a mechanism to cut off an inmate's communications with the outside world."

Prosecutors argued there was no way of ensuring the tight penal restrictions would continue for more than a few years. Prisoners often get restrictions lifted for good behavior, allowing them social visits with other inmates and the possibility of being transferred to less-restrictive institutions, according to prosecutors.

The defense saved their star witness for the last when they called Sister Helen Prejean, a Catholic nun, author and vociferous advocate against the death penalty.

After meeting Dzhokhar five times in jail, she declared him "absolutely" sorry from his crimes.

"He said it emphatically," she testified. "He said, 'No one deserves to suffer like they did.' I had every reason to believe that he was taking it in and was genuinely sorry for what he did."

Prejean was the first witness to testify on Dzhokhar's thoughts about the bombings.

She said he "kind of lowered his eyes" as he talked about the victims. "It had pain in it," she said.

Bombing victims in the audience shook their heads and looked as though they did not believe her testimony.

Prejean rose to fame as the author of the book "Dead Man Walking," which was made into a 1995 film adaptation. She sometimes has visited prisoners facing death penalties in her role as a nun.

With Dzhokhar, she discussed the difference between Catholicism and Islam and his feelings about the marathon bombings in a meeting she described as "pleasant."

"I'm not sure he'd ever met a nun before but he was very open and receptive," Prejean said.

During a brief cross-examination by the prosecution, she acknowledged her opposition to the death penalty might have influenced her opinion.

Afterward, both sides rested.

Before the jury began deliberating on May 13, prosecutors and defense attorneys made their last closing argument on the death penalty.

Judge O'Toole told the jurors, "The choice between these very serious alternatives is yours and yours alone."

The attorneys did not say anything new. They just said it more forcefully.

"The bombs burned their skin, shattered their bones and ripped their flesh," Prosecutor Steve Mellin said. "Merely killing the person isn't nearly as terrifying as shredding them apart."

He held up a photo to the jury showing Martin Richard and other children standing on a barricade near the marathon finish line moments before the bomb exploded. Then he showed a second large photo of the victims lying bloodied on the sidewalk.

"This is what terrorism looks like," Mellin said.

Dzhokhar's response to the bombings was selfish indifference, according to the prosecutor.

"This defendant does not want to die," Mellin said. "You know that because he had many opportunities to die on the streets of Boston and Watertown. But unlike his brother, he made a different choice. A death sentence is not giving him what he wants. It is giving him what he deserves."

Judy Clarke asked the jury to consider what Dzhokhar could become as he matured, not what he had done at the 2013 marathon. He was "the invisible kid" in the shadow of his "jihadi wannabe" brother, she said.

Sparing him from the death penalty would be "a decision of strength," Clarke said.

"Dzhokhar is not the worst of the worst, and that's what the death penalty is reserved for – the worst of the worst," Clarke said. Her client was "genuinely sorry for what he's done."

Prison instead of the death penalty would make him disappear into a life of being locked in a cell 23 hours a day. A life sentence "reflects justice and mercy," Clarke said. "Yes, even for the Boston Marathon bomber."

In mid-afternoon, the jury moved to the jury room to begin deliberating. They spoke among themselves for about 45 minutes before the judge dismissed them for the day.

The next day, the two questions they submitted to the judge

in notes made it anyone's guess where they were headed with a judgment.

In the first question, the jurors asked for a better definition of "aiding and abetting." They wanted to know whether it meant Dzhokhar personally intended to kill people with the marathon bombs or whether it meant he was still guilty if he was following directions from his brother.

Judge O'Toole discussed the question with the attorneys before responding by telling jurors to follow his earlier instructions and to let the evidence guide their decision-making.

The second question asked about filling out the 24-page verdict form. The judge again told them to follow his earlier instructions while reminding them that a death sentence must be unanimous.

The first full day of deliberation failed to end with a verdict. The jury needed one more day.

THE VERDICT

SHORTLY BEFORE 3 P.M. on Friday, May 15, 2015, CNN anchor Brooke Baldwin said on national television, "The world is watching Boston." A live camera showed the Moakley federal courthouse in the background.

At 3:10 p.m., the seven women and five men who had decided Dzhokhar's fate filed back into the courtroom and took their seats in the jury box. The forewoman handed the envelope to Judge O'Toole, who handed it to the clerk of the court.

It took the clerk 20 minutes to read each charge and the jury's answers to the questions in the 24-page verdict form. The answers showed the jury rejected nearly all the defense team's arguments during 14-1/2 hours of deliberations.

The clerk reached the death penalty questions toward the end of the form. On six of the 17 charges that could bring the death penalty, the jury decided Dzhokhar should be executed.

Dzhokhar gave no hint of emotion. He stood with his hands in front of himself. His head was bowed part of the time. He cracked his knuckles twice. He looked straight ahead as the death sentence was read.

No one in the audience – survivors, victims' families, news media – said a word. The judge warned everyone beforehand that any outbursts would be punished as contempt of court.

Many jurors appeared emotionally drained, a few close to tears. The verdict forms showed only three of the 12 jurors believed Dzhokhar was influenced by his brother to set the bombs. Only two jurors believed he was sorry for his actions.

The judge polled each of the jurors to ensure they agreed with the verdict read by the clerk. They all agreed. Afterward, the judge thanked Dzhokhar for behaving appropriately during the trial.

As federal marshals walked up to him to take him away to a detention cell, Dzhokhar smiled faintly with a wry smile. He made a quizzical motion with his hands at his hips that some people in the audience described as a "gunslinger's salute." He was then led away.

Outside the courthouse, the media was interviewing victims, attorneys and occasionally a man-on-the-street.

Karen Brassard, a marathon bombing survivor, said, "I know that there is still a long road ahead. There's going to be many, many, many more dates ahead but right now it feels like we can take a breath."

Liz Norden, whose two sons each lost a leg in the bombings, said, "I have to watch my two sons put a leg on every day so I don't know about closure. But I can tell you it feels like a weight has been lifted off my shoulders."

U.S. Attorney Carmen Ortiz said, "Today the jury has spoken and Dzhokhar Tsarnaev will pay with his life for his crimes. Make no mistake, the defendant claimed to be acting on behalf of all Muslims. This was not a religious crime and it certainly doesn't reflect true Muslim beliefs. It was a political crime designed to intimidate and to coerce the United States."

Legal commentators said the verdict was only the beginning of a much longer process. Survivors would be given an opportunity to tell the court how the bombings disrupted their lives, the judge would announce details of the punishment and years of appeals would follow. There was no doubt Dzhokhar would be executed by lethal injection at the federal penitentiary in Terre Haute, Indiana. The only question was how long it would take.

Whether it was sooner or later, the more important issue was that an Islamic terrorist had been sentenced to death at a time of rising lone wolf threats.

A week earlier, FBI Director James Comey announced there are "hundreds, maybe thousands" of Islamic fundamentalist sympathizers in the United States being recruited by terrorist groups.

ISIS was using Twitter and other social media to push "disturbed people" over the brink into violence, Comey said. "It's like the devil sitting on their shoulders, saying 'kill, kill, kill,'" Comey said at a press conference.

Meanwhile, the FBI was investigating a foiled ISIS attack in Garland, Texas on May 3, 2015. Two ISIS sympathizers outraged by the right wing American Freedom Defense Initiative's sponsorship of an art contest for cartoon images of the prophet Mohammed tried to shoot into a crowd of about 200 people. Images of the prophet are forbidden by Islamic doctrine. The group was offering a $10,000 prize for the best cartoon.

Both of the attackers were shot and killed by a police officer as they opened fire. One man was shot in the ankle but treated and released from a local hospital.

Stopping the Garland attack did nothing to prevent larger risks posed by ISIS' sophisticated recruiting strategy for lone wolf terrorism, according to the FBI. Unlike other terrorist organizations, ISIS did not organize the attacks with top-down planning that could be tracked by U.S. intelligence agencies. Instead, they merely inspire attacks and provide information over the Internet on how to succeed with them.

In other words, their modus operandi was a nearly perfect example of the bombings by Tamerlan and Dzhokhar Tsarnaev and the shooting at Garland.

ISIS claimed responsibility for the Garland attack and issued a warning broadcast over a Raqqa, Syria radio station that was translated by the Associated Press.

"We tell ... America that what is coming will be more grievous and more bitter and you will see from the soldiers of the caliphate what will harm you, God willing," the message said.

For potential recruits with more than curiosity about ISIS, the group steers them to encrypted websites based in Syria where their communications are "lost to us," Comey said.

"The haystack is the entire country," Comey said. "We are looking for the needles, but increasingly the needles are unavailable to us." Some of the "needles" consist of mobile phones carried in the pockets of suspects.

Hundreds of cases of potential homegrown terrorism are being investigated by all 56 of the FBI's field divisions, he said.

Days before Dzhokhar was sentenced to death, the U.S. military raised its threat level at its North American bases. The increase from Alpha to Bravo on the four-level threat scale was not prompted by a single event, merely higher risks posed by terrorist groups. Alpha is the lowest threat level.

Questions lingered about whether more random bag and vehicle checks at military bases with the higher threat level would do much to stop ISIS.

Questions also lingered about what the Boston jury accomplished by sentencing Dzhokhar Tsarnaev to death.

"This punishment only continues the cycle of violence and it will not bring peace," Jay Parini, a Vermont poet and novelist, wrote in a commentary published by CNN. "In fact, the execution of Tsarnaev will transform him into a martyr and millions around the world will find fresh reasons to dislike the United States."

The Tsarnaevs' bombings were rooted in the Sept. 11, 2001 terrorist attack and the U.S.-led war in Iraq and Afghanistan that killed more than 100,000 people.

"Of course, it was impossible to know the full extent of the terror that would follow and that indeed ISIS would rush in to fill a vacuum created by wiping out Saddam's army," Parini wrote. "Violence follows violence.

"From this, angry, distorted men, like the Tsarnaev brothers, drew justification for their unspeakable actions.

"Cycles of violence are difficult, nearly impossible, to break."

www.ingramcontent.com/pod-product-compliance
Lightning Source LLC
Chambersburg PA
CBHW020407080526
44584CB00014B/1216